STYLING *for* ENTERTAINING

12 MIRACLE MAKEOVERS,
8 SIMPLE STEPS

SUSIE COELHO

PHOTOGRAPHS BY BOBBI FABIAN

ALSO BY SUSIE COELHO
SUSIE COELHO'S EVERYDAY STYLING

SIMON & SCHUSTER

NEW YORK   LONDON   TORONTO   SYDNEY   SINGAPORE

SIMON & SCHUSTER
ROCKEFELLER CENTER
1230 AVENUE OF THE AMERICAS
NEW YORK NY 10020

For information about special discounts for bulk purchases,
please contact Simon & Schuster Special Sales at
1-800-456-6798 or business@simonandschuster.com.

Designed by Madeleine Corson Design, San Francisco

Manufactured in the United States of America

10 9 8 7 6 5 4 3 2 1

Library of Congress Cataloging-in-Publication Data

Coelho, Susie.
    Styling for entertaining: twelve miracle makeovers, eight easy steps/
 Susie Coelho; photographs by Bobbi Fabian.
    p. cm.
    1. Entertaining. 2. Interior decoration. 3. Table setting and decoration. 4. Cookery.
    5. Handicraft. I. Title: Styling for entertaining. II. Title.

TX731.C615 2003
747—dc21   2003052811

ISBN 0-7432-4662-4

To Bobby, Hutton, and Hailey—

for loving me, imperfections and all, and for being here for me to love.

CONTENTS

THE PATIO 108

THE LAWN 148

PREFACE

I was born to a life of styling—literally.

My parents lived in England at the time, and their neighbors, who soon became friends, wanted to throw an Indian dinner soiree. So my mother, never a believer in halfway measures and not about to let the fact that she was nine months pregnant stand in her way, volunteered to help cook the dinner one snowy night—curry, dahl, rice, chapatis, even puris from scratch. She was rolling out the puris when I decided I just couldn't wait any longer to join the party. And join it I did, right after the arrival of a last-minute invitee, the obstetrician.

Later, when our family moved to Washington, D. C., my mother started working for a Latin American organization, and soon she was serving paella—the Spanish risotto that calls for a dizzying shopping list of fresh seafood, chicken, chorizo, mussels, saffron, and so on—and teaching us the Spanish she'd learned at work.

After another move, this time to Paris, she enrolled at the Alliance Française to learn the language and all things French. Before we knew it, quiches and crêpes were flying from kitchen to dining room table. I'll never forget the day she turned the crêpe pan over to me. I was mixing flour with fleur d'oranger (the secret ingredient in making great crêpes) with grand aplomb. I was officially the head chef, at least on Sunday!

I could get philosophical and start talking about integrating the parts of one's life into a synergistic whole, but my mom took a simpler view: This is your life, so jump right in. She never tiptoed through life, hoping not to cause a fuss.

She had a gift for inspiring the same attitude in others. I especially remember during one summer vacation, when my mother extended her gift to an Australian girl traveling by herself through the South of France. She was lonely, and hungry—hungry for someone to speak English with, and for the kinds of food she ate at home. My mom invited her to tag along with us and immediately began to teach her a few vital French words and phrases. We made a game of speaking only French and scrambling for the dictionary—in the process building vocabulary and confidence. Step by step, my mother gently introduced the girl to the joys of French cuisine; after all, is it really such a big leap from fried chicken to coq au vin? By the time we had to part company and head home, the girl had finally stepped into the world of the French, and was loving it. All thanks to my mother.

My mother was always styling her life, my life, and the lives of those around her. The way she saw it, your world is what you make of it, and the more you create, the more you have to enjoy—and to give. And the more she could help open the doors and windows of the world for others, the happier she was.

I feel blessed that I inherited my mother's joie de vivre, her energy, and most of all her joy in helping others. For a long time I didn't feel fulfilled in life, and only started to after I turned a pivotal corner. I was wondering how my mother would think in my shoes, and I realized that she wouldn't be asking what she wanted from life, but what others needed from her. Thank you, Mom, for helping me fulfill my dreams and find my purpose in life. 🪷

STYLING

SIMPLE S

IN 8
TEPS

You know the saying: If you want to whip your house into shape or even just get the place clean, throw a party! For some reason, hosting a bash has the power to evoke styling inspiration in each of us. It seems that as soon as you decide to invite people over, you suddenly have the eyes of a designer, the spirit of a magician, and the energy of third-graders on a playground—or at least you wish you did!

STYLING IN 8 SIMPLE STEPS

A step-by-step system that will get you styling like a professional in no time.

WHY DOES THE MERE PROSPECT OF THROWING a party excite us into action after we've gone weeks or months without so much as buying new dish towels for the kitchen? For one thing, most of us are energized by the challenge of creating a special environment for a special occasion, for nothing gets a party going like the right atmosphere. For another, once you decide to have a party, the drive kicks in to make it a standout—something to talk about. Not only do we want our guests to have a great time, we also hope that at the end of the evening they'll walk away with smiles on their faces and say, "What a party! What a house! How does she do it?" But perhaps most importantly, fixing up the home in anticipation of guests is a creative act, an avenue of personal expression. And that's what styling for entertaining is all about.

Styling for Entertaining will help you develop your own personal style so you can entertain more with less effort, enjoy every moment to the fullest, and reap the many benefits of living in a welcoming, creative space. Everyone has their own story about why they entertain less than they'd like. Mine was that I began a demanding new career at about the same time that I became a mom. Wow, did things change! One of my largest styling dilemmas was the dining room, which I'd converted into a playroom for the baby. Hmm, where to put grown-up people wanting something to eat? I had previously co-owned two restaurants, so the utter absence of a dining table presented a whole new challenge. My child's needs unquestionably came first, but *I* still wanted to entertain. I needed to streamline and simplify—reduce the stress, get maximum effect from a minimal outlay of time and money, and then make sure that I was having as much fun as my guests.

My solution was an easy-access approach to creating fabulous spaces to entertain in based on the principles of Everyday Styling that I introduced in my first book.

Styling is a relatively simple and inexpensive process that can almost immediately give your home and garden a new personality. It does not require much more than your own creativity. Simply by looking at things in a fresh light, you can manipulate your spaces and turn them into beautiful sanctuaries and relaxing retreats. Because the commitment of time and money is significantly less than when you decorate or landscape, you can allow yourself to experiment to no end. When you style you use your own creativity, rearranging your belongings in a fresh new way, rather than using someone else's cookie-cutter design. You can easily update your spaces once you look at them as an opportunity to express your personality and your lifestyle, and to unearth your inherent creativity. Anyone can style on any budget. That's the allure of styling!

Certain spaces are central to opening up your home for easy entertaining. Your living room should welcome guests to sit back and relax; your dining room should easily morph into different styles for varying menus; your patio should be a comfortable environment that offers the best of indoors and out; and your backyard lawn should be able to transform instantly for outdoor events.

In my experience working makeovers on hundreds of homes, I've found that these four areas—living room, dining room, patio, and lawn—are not only places where most people entertain, but also areas where homeowners say they need the most help.

fluent in styling each an endless variety of your fingertips."

Waiting to be discovered within these four areas, like sculptures hidden in stone before the artist begins carving, are many different party settings. These few spaces can give you enough flexibility for all kinds of get-togethers—from tea for two to a buffet for dozens of people. Becoming fluent in styling each area will put an endless variety of parties at your fingertips.

The style of any space in your home can change as naturally as the seasons or with your mood, and change is both practical and creative. On one hand, your

"...your home also craves attention—and what better excuse for a makeover than to throw a party?"

entertaining venues have to shift from one function to another to serve the purposes and particulars of the event. On the other, any space looks and feels stale if it stays the same for too long. Just as your plants need water, fertilizer, light, and an occasional haircut in order to blossom and grow, your home also craves attention—and what better excuse for a makeover than to throw a party?

By the way, my styling solution to the missing dining room was to have a table made for the living room—my favorite room in the house, with its beautiful fireplace and hand-painted 1927 wood coffer ceiling. During the day, this French country farm table doubles as a beautiful desk (complete with a fake drawer), while for special dinners it opens up with leaves and seats twelve with ease. I love our fireside parties in our customized "dining" room! ⚶

STYLING FOR ENTERTAINING

By bringing together ideas from the worlds of professional entertaining and styling, I've stream-lined the process of styling for entertaining into eight simple and reliable steps that make both the creative and logistical parts of a party doable and fun. Whether you enjoy elaborate affairs, prefer to keep your get-togethers simple, or want to change effects with every event or season, the eight steps provide a blueprint you can follow every time.

To illustrate the eight steps in action, I've created twelve makeovers for entertaining you'll see in the following chapters, each accomplished by following the same procedure. None of the make-overs take more than a day or two, even those that require building structures or repainting furniture. That's the power of having a system. And if the mere idea of a makeover has you groaning and giving up before you start, don't worry: the eight steps make it easy. When the procedure is predictable, you can unleash your imagination and embrace the surprises styling for entertaining brings.

So check the calendar. Grab a notepad and pen. You're about to learn a process that will keep you styling for life!

I WHAT IS THE OCCASION? A friend of mine planning a birthday party for her small twin boys thought it would be fun to add an elegant cocktail party for the young guests' parents. Location: their big living room, with ice cream and cake at one table, champagne, cocktails, and canapés at another. Sounds fun and different, right? But my friend didn't think the idea all the way through. Twenty running, squirming, sugared-up five-year-olds with sticky hands and faces, plus expensive suits and dresses, plus tall slender glassware standing atop the perfect setting for a fort or playhouse, equals . . . Let us now draw the curtain on the next morning's bottleneck at the dry cleaners.

The question, "What's the occasion?" seems so simplemindedly obvious that we too often forget to ask it. But all of your creative choices stem from the answer, so let's give it some thought.

Why are you entertaining? Is it your best friend's birthday? Time to have a few friends over for cocktails? Did you just decide to host your son's wedding in your own backyard? Or maybe you simply want to restyle the patio because spring has come, or spruce up the living room to give yourself a change. Defining the occasion gives meaning to your plans, so think through what you're celebrating and why. Whatever the reason, write it down now.

2 ENVISION YOUR IDEAL SETTING With the groundwork laid, now is your chance to dream. What is the most exhilarating environment you can imagine? Let your mind soar with ideas. Do you want a romantic, flowery garden filled with the sweet aroma of English roses—a perfect setting for afternoon tea with a close friend? Or are you captivated by the idea of creating a desert oasis in your backyard, with luxurious lounging areas and passionate colors where you can serve exotic foods and relax on a summer evening?

ASIAN FUSION
STYLE BOARD
MATERIALS

🔺 Miscellaneous colorful food packages

🔺 Origami paper

🔺 Artificial cherry blossoms and orchids

🔺 Mint green paper napkins

🔺 Plastic spoon

🔺 Bamboo sushi roll

🔺 Chopsticks

🔺 Tea bags

🔺 String of beads

🔺 Top of the teapot

🔺 Candies in colorful packages

🔺 Handwritten menu

🔺 Paper kimono from a gift card

This step requires you to frame a big picture of the space in your mind. If you're short on ideas, try paging through your favorite magazines and books, or preview Step 3 to spark the seeds of your vision. If the first image that comes to mind doesn't seem to fit your home or garden—perhaps a ten-foot waterfall is a bit extravagant for your allocated space and budget— then find a substitute that incorporates its essence, such as a small water feature. At this stage, don't second-guess yourself by thinking you can't reach your goal because of budget or time. Believe me, I know how easy it is to get stuck in the practical logistics from the very start. How many chairs do I need? How many plates? How much wine? How many manicures for all the nail biting? Quiet these chattering voices and take this opportunity to expand your styling possibilities beyond the boundaries your skeptical mind tries to draw. Keep working your image until it becomes clear, and you can't wait to get started.

In this step, you will also need to determine the location. This decision isn't as straightforward as it sounds. A large dinner party might work better in a living room than in the dining room, while a formal tea you'd thought to hold in the living room could be even more elegant in the backyard. Take into account the number of guests you're inviting and what kind of event it will be, then consider all four spaces—living room, dining room, patio, and yard—before choosing the best location. Once you've determined where you will be entertaining, your makeover will be much more tangible, as you have finally set its physical framework.

3 DEVELOP A MAKEOVER STYLE   Now that you have a vision, you need to take the image from your head and make it manifest in the physical world by determining your style. The style is the overall general concept that will guide your makeover to fruition. It will focus you, and your styling supplies, and give you a clear concept that will make it easy to weed out the yesses from the nos. Think of words that you can use to describe a style for your makeover— tropical, vintage, ethnic, Asian—and I'm sure just the words themselves have already given you a feeling or picture in your head.

Now, come up with a title: "Tropical Paradise," "Vintage Romance," "Exotic Oasis," or "Asian Fusion." You have suddenly created your own makeover style. You can find inspiration for your makeover style in a seasonal holiday or particular event, a single inspirational item, a photo you saw in a magazine, or even something as intangible as a memory of good times past, ripe for revisiting and creative play. So check your box of treasures under the bed, or an old scrapbook from your last vacation for inspiration. Don't worry if your style idea is not fully developed at this point; it will become more clear in the steps to come. It's always better to make a decision and move forward (especially if it doesn't cost you anything) than to wallow in indecision—the kiss of death for an artist.

4 CREATE YOUR STYLE BOARD   In this step you begin to bring the makeover style to life and refine it through work with your Style Board. You'll collect and display the materials that move you into action: pictures, color samples, and other items that align with your style, mood, and color. Although creating a Style Board isn't essential for every entertaining makeover, it is, nonetheless, an extremely beneficial tool when styling. Designers often assemble such boards for their clients with samples of tile, fabric, and drawings to test ideas and serve as a creative springboard. Likewise, creating a Style Board allows you to find real-life examples that illustrate the ideas you have in your head. It's like a scrapbook of an event that hasn't yet occurred; a transfer of ideas from your imagination into visible reality.

To create your Style Board, buy a piece of white or colored foam core from an art-supply or craft store or a framing shop. This light, sturdy, and inexpensive material makes a handy medium for playing with style ideas and is easy to move from room to room. Start by pasting, tacking, or sticking small items to the board that have inspired your style. These may include fabric swatches, small ornaments or accessories, paint samples, tear sheets from magazines, pictures from your Style File (see "Style File," p. 20), and recipes and food photos that fan the creative flame. Keep an eye out for snippets in your daily rounds—bits of ribbon or lace, wrapping paper or seed packages, stickers, matchbook covers.

BELOW *Style Board for Asian Fusion*

The Style Board enables you to try out colors and ideas for your makeover before you make the commitment of time and money. Experiment; swap things around; add and discard. Don't hesitate to return to your Style Board at any point as you find new materials or test and develop new ideas. You may have no problem coming up with a color palette in this step, but if you do, it is perfectly okay to revisit your Style Board for color refinement later in the eight-step process.

STYLE FILE

The Style File, a powerful creative tool I introduced in my first book, *Everyday Styling,* helps you whip up a Style Board in no time flat. Essentially, the Style File is a collection of images you like—colors, patterns, designs, rooms, gardens, and so on. Once you learn how to collect and work with the visual images that inspire you, your styling possibilities are endless.

Here's a quick route to creating your personal Style File:
• Label four file folders "Indoors," "Outdoors," "Holidays," and "What Were They Thinking?"
• Take some time to look through magazines, books, and catalogs, pulling out anything that favorably impresses you: flower arrangements, table settings, color combinations, living room setups, dinnerware, deck treatments, holiday decorations. Mark each picture with the date, then circle the part that attracts you and write a note about why ("pretty flower arrangement," "russet and gold color combo"). For the "What Were They Thinking?" file, pull images you don't like or that just plain make you wonder who would design such a thing? Sometimes knowing what you don't like helps build confidence in what you do. File the pictures into the four folders as you go.
• Continue to collect pictures until you have a good assortment, then organize them one step further. In a file drawer, accordion file, or portable file box, label four hanging files with the four main categories, then insert file folders for subcategories: individual rooms for the "Indoors" file; each of the holidays you hope to celebrate; the patio, lawn, kids' areas, garden, and so forth for the "Outdoors" file. You don't need subcategories for "What Were They Thinking?"
• Keep adding photos, clippings, and printouts to your Style File, and you'll soon have an archive of your personal preferences, a practical guide to your own taste, and a rich trove of ideas for all your styling projects.

5 PAINT YOUR COLOR PALETTE A carefully chosen and consistent color palette is probably the most important aspect of successful styling, whether for entertaining or for any other makeover. A well-conceived color scheme creates visual flow and balance in any space.

Choosing the color palette for a party can be a little different from other styling steps in that there are special considerations above and beyond personal preference. A wedding, for example,

LEFT *Tropical Style Board*

TAKE YOUR COLOR PALETTE FROM YOUR STYLE BOARD

The basis of your color palette is derived from your Style Board. Shown is the Candy Cane Christmas Style Board, which is a simple red and white color scheme. You can see how the makeover starts to take form as decisions are made throughout the creating of the board. You might refine your colors from a red burgundy to a brighter fresher red. This change will change the supplies you use and define the direction of the makeover before you start. The style board allows you to make mistakes that don't cost you time or money!

almost always calls for a certain amount of white. Season and tradition affect color selection, from the reds and greens of Christmas to the pastel shades of spring. For a special-occasion makeover, you may decide to use bolder colors than you normally would, knowing that you can tone them down when the party's over.

The basis of your color palette will most likely come from your Style Board. (In some cases you might already have a color palette in mind from the occasion you settled on in Step 1.) Your palette may be obvious. If you've pinned up photos of daffodils, daisies, and sunflowers, a fresh yellow is clearly part of your palette. On the other hand, you may need to study your Style Board for a while before understanding its theme. A collage of country-style living rooms may seem like a cacophony of disparate colors until the common element emerges: simple pieces painted white. Move items around to create different color combinations until your palette announces itself. After you've decided on your colors, give each one a name that helps support your overall makeover style. If your makeover is based on a patriotic theme, don't just use red, white, and blue. Try Apple Red, Picket-Fence White, and True Blue. It will help to get you in the spirit of things and jazz up your overall makeover.

In general, pastel colors tend to soften and blend. Neutrals—unobtrusive whites and off-whites, beiges, and grays—are easy to work with, as you can add accents of color anytime. Bright colors make a bold statement and bring vibrant energy to a room or space. What to do if you're stuck with colors that you don't love—like that red floral sofa you haven't yet figured out how to replace? Try working them into your palette to harmonize with the whole, or simply cover them up. There's nothing like a throw to brighten that drab old olive chair!

6 GATHER YOUR STYLING SUPPLIES   Now that your vision, makeover style, and Style Board have determined your direction, it's time to go shopping—but not in the traditional sense. The first step in gathering your styling supplies is to shop your house. That's right; grab a basket or empty box and start ransacking each room for anything you can use in your makeover. If your color palette is yellow and green, pull everything you find in those colors even if you don't yet know how you'll use them. If it's a tea garden you're creating, look for teacups and saucers, silver teapots and plates, wide-brimmed hats, and anything related to roses. Don't overlook the neglected spots around the house, for that's often where the good stuff hides. Basements, attics, garages, sheds, storage areas, high shelves and cabinets, the tops, backs, and bottoms of closets. These are your forgotten treasure troves. Even the kids' rooms are fair game!

Don't censor yourself at this point; grab everything, whether it usually serves a decorative role or not. Remember, there's no price tag when you shop your own house. Only after you've completed your sweep should you assemble everything in one spot, on a table or floor, and review your collection. What you're looking for now are the items that seem to gravitate toward each other, because they're in a similar or coordinating color palette, or support your theme, or create a surprising combination you like. If something looks odd or out of place, take it away. Don't even question why. You can always use it in another makeover. Styling never stops!

After shopping the house, start a list of items you're missing—maybe a few dishes, a rug for under the sofa, fresh flowers for the table. (Some needs will be obvious now, while others will crop up as you start styling. Just be sure to write everything down.) These are the items you'll need to buy, borrow, or substitute. If you find that you have to buy too much, consider adjusting your color palette or adding another shade so you can use more styling supplies you already have.

In any case, with a concise list, the shopping trip for your makeover should be short and financially sweet. Professional stylists never go shopping without a very specific list; otherwise it would cost the client a fortune and many hours while they perused the shops looking for inspiration. Make your main decisions *before* you hit the stores—though you can always keep your eyes open for that brilliant last-minute addition.

Vintage Romance began with the basic foundation shown here. Each makeover will start with a foundation. Keep in mind the type of event you are preparing for while placing your furniture, as this will help you determine the proper placement. Don't worry if you can't figure it out immediately—you may be halfway through the styling process when you realize you just have to move the sofa to the other side of the room. Like everything else, play with the arrangement until it feels just right. You may find furniture in other rooms—don't be afraid to borrow from the rest of the house.

7 STYLE THE SPACE   With your styling supplies now on hand, you're ready for action! It's time to style the space. Because this is the crucial juncture where your vision comes to life, I've broken Step 7 down into three sub-steps. This sequence will help your styling go faster and will soon become second nature as you gain confidence in your ability to do it over and over with different results each time. (Warning: Styling can be addictive!)

LAY THE FOUNDATION   The best styling starts with a clean slate. Yes, that means moving everything but your furniture out of the room or off the patio for your makeover. If there are any pieces you know will not work for the particular makeover style you have chosen, move them out now. If you aren't sure at this point if a certain piece of furniture will work or not, leave it in the room. Through the process of styling, you will easily be able to determine what stays and what goes. Although this may seem like a lot of unnecessary work, believe me, it will save you extra effort later on. Think of it this way: you're an artist, and you should start your magnum opus with an empty canvas.

Once the area is cleared, lay the foundation and place the furniture. Indoors, the large items to arrange include sofas, coffee tables, side tables, armchairs, hutches or armoires, and dining tables. Outdoors, place patio tables or lawn furniture, benches, arbors or fencing, large water features or fountains. Large items also include specially built structures for outdoor makeovers such as a gazebo, arbors, or canopy frames—anything that will provide a foundation or frame for your makeover.

Work with the largest items first. As you go, take into account the number of guests, possible traffic flow, and how much seating you'll need. Do you want people to serve themselves from both sides of the buffet table? How about a separate table for the kids? Do you want some open space for speeches, games, or performances, or instead need to close up the room into a cozy nook for an intimate occasion? Foresee fast mid-event changes, say, from dining to dancing, and figure out how you'll make them. In short, envision the space filled with guests and the activities you plan, and ask yourself if your setup allows everyone to comfortably drink, eat, converse, and circulate. You'll want to ensure your setup won't create a bottleneck where people crash into each other trying to get past the sofa to reach the hors d'oeuvres!

I don't like rules that say how you have to place your furniture. No single set of principles accommodates all situations and tastes. Rules also squelch personal expression and reduce your chance of coming up with something original. Instead, I prefer to move the furniture around, try different approaches, and experiment until it feels right. Not only does this hands-on approach yield an arrangement tailored to your event, but moving pieces around is also how you learn which looks you like the best. And hey, it's good exercise.

SOFTEN THE LINES Now that the foundation is in place, the next task is to place the styling items that soften the look. Indoor styling supplies include area rugs, fabric wall hangings and curtains, paintings or artwork, pillows, tablecloths, and throws. Outdoor items include plants, fabric for the arbor, and some of the same soft items you might use inside, such as rugs, pillows, throws, or tablecloths. Some styling projects will fall into this phase if they pertain to softening the space—making a painting, decorative screen, wrapping-paper collage, or fabric wall hanging or framing a piece of antique clothing.

As you style in this phase, work with what you have before running out to buy what you think is missing. If you don't like the color of the sofa, you can first try changing it with an old bedspread before investing in a brand-new throw. Do the chairs need a pick-me-up? Add a bright pillow to one and a slipcover to another. Outdoors, use the plants you have to soften walls, pillars, and walkways. Tall vines in containers highlight the wood frame of an arbor or a fence, a cluster of potted flowering plants define and brighten a garden path, and a trio of miniature fruit trees masks a garage wall.

PERSONALIZE WITH DETAILS As much work as we do arranging furniture and creating the overall style of a space or event, it's the small touches that other people most often notice and remember. Invaluable in personalizing a space and defining your own signature style, the details may come toward the end of the process but should still take top priority. Whether you finish your look with a group of specially selected photos on the piano, mismatched vintage dishes to serve your bistro dinner, a patio buffet strewn with tropical flowers, or strings of tiny white lights to give shape to trees and bushes on the lawn, these small details speak volumes and set the mood.

At this stage of styling, I like to bring all the small items into the room and quickly place them here and there, letting my first instincts guide me. Then I step back, look at the effect, and begin to assess and adjust. Too much thinking right off the bat can forestall the creative process. So don't micromanage. Act with abandon!

SOFTEN WITH PILLOWS

Pillows are an excellent softening tool and are a key element in supporting your color palette.

Once you've got a first pass in place, look at the space from both a wide-angle point of view, by standing in the doorway or entrance, and from close up, sitting on the sofa and gazing at the items on the coffee table. Decide whether something's missing, or if a tabletop seems too cluttered or a tall vase blocks a view. Now adjust and fine-tune until everything feels just right.

You might delete some accessories if you're going for a clean, modern look. If, instead, an eclectic feel is your goal, try shuffling your styling supplies around to discover more surprising combinations. Grouping items in threes is always a good idea, as is grouping together different shapes that share a common element, such as color or texture. Generally, it is best to put taller items in the back, and smaller items toward the front. These styling tips go for flower arrangements as well. For a more formal effect, however, strike a note of symmetry and balance by placing two matching candlesticks on a mantle or two potted ficus trees to define an entrance.

Once everything seems to be in place, step back and take a fresh, critical look. Have you realized your vision? If not, anything is open to change, even that second sofa you lugged in that you now see takes up too much space. Don't think you've failed if something doesn't work. Assessing and adjusting are simply another stage of the creative process. All artists do it!

8 STYLE THE FOOD AND TABLE This final step to styling for entertaining includes finalizing the menu, setting the table, preparing and styling the food. The on-the-spot logistics of entertaining become seamless when you have a plan complete with a preparation schedule and serving pieces, dishware, and table linens picked out and ready to go.

At most gatherings, the food and drink are of primary importance, yet it's easy to lapse into a just-get-it-finished mindset here. So often the food is ready but you're wondering, Where's the tablecloth? Do I have enough glasses and plates? Do I use paper or cloth napkins? Avoid the common pitfall of concentrating merely on what's being served, and start to think about *how* it will be served. Styling for entertaining means incorporating your food and table into the styling process. Once you start recognizing the food and drink as styling accessories, you will notice that the inherent colors, flavors, and cultural history of the dishes on the menu provide infinite opportunities to underscore your style.

Styling the food and the table can make a big difference to your guests, who will feel indulged by your attention to detail. A simple plate of pasta doesn't seem at all ho-hum when it's offered in a rustic Tuscan pasta bowl and garnished artfully with freshly shaved Parmesan and fragrant leaves of basil. Homemade spring rolls are so much more fun when you playfully present them in white take-out boxes. If you're serving cookies for dessert, don't just slap them on a plate; sculpt a pyramid, stud it with truffles, and sift a light snow of powdered sugar around the plate's edge. Playing with colors, shapes, and garnishes can turn your menu into a work of art—and when your personal style makes it to the table, your entertaining will be a success long after the last bite.

"...the joys of artistic expression."

A Puzzle Free Formula

Keeping the eight steps in mind, you're ready to turn the pages, enjoy the sample makeovers, and get started on your own. You'll find that these steps become second nature. Think of them as a dance routine—basic moves that flow into one another naturally and in a rhythm that changes with each song. Soon you'll become fluent with the steps, crafting each occasion with exuberance and grace. Don't worry if on one occasion you have a color palette in mind long before you reach Step 5, and on another day you change your mind about the location just as you start to place furniture. Just go with the flow and don't interrupt the creative process. Allow the artist within you to take over and adjust as you see fit.

Also, remember that although entertaining gives us a great reason to style our homes, you don't need a party or special occasion to get your space together. Why not start thinking of the home as a place where you will entertain frequently, and style those spaces with that thought in mind? Your home will inevitably

> **"Think of a dance routine—basic moves that flow into one another naturally..."**

become more vibrant, welcoming, and warm every day of the year. You will easily be able to throw both scheduled get-togethers and spontaneous, spur-of-the-moment gatherings with ease. And once you've opened up areas of the house and yard to welcome guests and parties, you can more easily go the extra distance when a big event or holiday calls for something special.

In the pages to come, I've styled each of the four key home areas in three different ways—for casual entertaining, for a seasonal celebration, and for a special event. This four-times-three formula covers all of your entertaining needs and multiplies into an endless array of fabulously styled events. Even when you're not entertaining, styling with the anticipation of creating a welcoming environment for your guests makes your home more comfortable and enjoyable year round. When you style, you unleash your creativity and allow yourself to endlessly experience the joys of artistic expression.

THE LIVING

R O O M

CHAPTER 2

🪷

Why do so many parties start in the

living room and end up in the kitchen

or the hallway or spilling outside onto

the deck? Maybe it's because so many

living rooms are pristine shrines to

their owner's good taste—beautifully

decorated perhaps, but not quite

right for good times.

These makeovers do away with the

stuffy living room forever and show how

one room can have many faces—from

sleekly modern to merrily seasonal to

romantically feminine—without a major

investment of time or money.

DESERT MODERN

BEFORE

AFTER

CANDY CANE CHRISTMAS

BEFORE

AFTER

VINTAGE ROMANCE

BEFORE

AFTER

In my everyday makeover "Desert Modern" I show how you can enjoy all the character and glamour of a period style—here, 1950s modern—without paying period prices or becoming a serious collector. If you start by window-shopping at high-end stores, you can learn to isolate elements of the style—geometric shapes, unexpected angles, and simple lines. ✿ The same room that seems so thoroughly modern and chic can brim with holiday cheer via the seasonal "Candy Cane Christmas" makeover. This quick transformation takes the stress out of holiday decorating and turns the living room into a child's **red-and-white fantasy.** If your holiday routines are getting stale, you'll enjoy the presents-and-breakfast setup here and use my system for categorizing and editing your decorations by color and theme to create fresh effects year after year. ✿ Are you ready to see your living room in a whole new light? Turn it into a **backstage boudoir** to celebrate a special—and grown-up—occasion. My "Vintage Romance" makeover calls for filling the room with armfuls of flowers, covering the furniture with laces and pretty fabrics, and decorating with artful creations. By bringing in items from elsewhere in the house—a vanity table, clothes, bedspreads, and throws—you style the room into a **seductive salon** you might love so much you'll live in it long after party day.

DESERT MODERN

This retro chic makeover results in a room that's as perennially stylish as a martini.

IMAGINE YOURSELF AT A CHIC COCKTAIL PARTY, WEARING A SASSY BLACK DRESS, DISCUSSING ART AND JAZZ WITH A MYSTERIOUS STRANGER. A stack of vinyl records sits by the hi-fi; cool grooves fill the room. The air buzzes with excitement. You nod knowingly and gently nibble the olive from your martini.

When we say "modern," we hark back to the sleek, spare, sophisticated look of the late '50s and early '60s. Fascination with the future was at an all-time high, and stars commissioned weekend homes in Palm Springs by popular architects such as Neutra, Cody, and Schindler. This Mid-Century Modern style is now back in full swing and easy to create on any budget.

So search your thrift stores or swanky boutiques and refresh your living room with a look that's both nostalgic and contemporary.

DUSTY TAUPE modern **sophisticated** desert sand

DESERT MODERN

1 WHAT IS THE OCCASION?   Entertaining business associates and friends for cocktails.

2 ENVISION YOUR IDEAL SETTING   An open furniture arrangement for easy mingling in the living room, allowing guests to sit or stand while enjoying drinks and hors d'oeuvres. The look should be modern and sleek, without too many items cluttering the space.

3 DEVELOP A MAKEOVER STYLE   Borrowing from past eras is a time-honored way to bring character to a room and also create a look that is entirely new. Entertaining with cocktails suggested the 1950s and '60s to me, so I decided to go all the way and work with a "Desert Modern" style for this makeover.

GROUPINGS OF THREE

Create an interesting vignette with a grouping of three items in various textures and shapes—such as a soft white feather in a small white vase, a Plexiglas geometric lamp, and a small square box all sitting on top of a round table.

earthy hues cocktail shaker mid-century

4 CREATE YOUR STYLE BOARD   A black-and-white photo from a magazine of an interior design from the early 1960s started my Style Board. I found it in my Style File along with other reference photos of furniture from that period. I filled the board with lots of geometric shapes from squares to circles. I also started playing around with colors and textures. From a housewares catalog, I tore out a photo of some elegant martini glasses and a cocktail shaker and added it to the board.

5 PAINT YOUR COLOR PALETTE   Three key pieces of furniture, a sofa, chair, and coffee table, already inhabited the room I was making over. Since each had clean, straight lines and was in a neutral color—beige, taupe, and dark brown—that fit this style, I decided to build from there. I used Desert Sand, Stone White, Dusty Taupe, and Chocolate Brown as a departure point for a palette of earthy desert hues.

STYLING SUPPLY LIST

Sofa

Dark coffee table

Glass side table

Round side table

Shag rug

Brown glass lamp

Large painting

Handmade wallpaper art

Throw pillows in geometric shapes

Modern Lucite lamp and a blown glass lamp from thrift store

Stainless steel cocktail shaker set

Martini glasses

Square textured white plates

Cocktail napkins

Geometric shaped vases

A few stems of greens

Puzzle

Feather

Books

6 GATHER YOUR STYLING SUPPLIES   Though this makeover may be retro, it doesn't require months of looking for authentic period items in antique shops. Chances are that you can quickly find a few 1950s pieces at secondhand shops—you'd be surprised how many end up at the Goodwill! If you have some simple, straight-lined furniture like a couch in a neutral color or rectangular tables, you're already on your way. Or you might look for some inexpensive pieces (old or new) like a canvas butterfly chair or one of molded plastic. Vases and old lamps are also easy to find; look for pieces that have interesting geometric shapes (circles, octagons, triangles) in the right colors. I gathered Japanese sushi plates because I liked their minimalist rectangle and

contrasting textures **abstract** geometric shapes

square shapes as well as their textures. I found an abstract puzzle that I used as an hors d'oeuvre place mat because its colors were so perfect. The shag rug, an important but inexpensive touch, is an easily found novelty item. And if you can't find a large piece of artwork within your budget, get hip, get modern, go wild, and make your own!

7 STYLE THE SPACE

LAY THE FOUNDATION To break away from the traditional placement of furniture around the fireplace and create a more open space for guests to mingle, I boldly moved the sofa in front of the fireplace; this setup works especially well during the spring or summer months when making a fire isn't on the top of your list. A chair set at an angle on one side of the sofa and an end table at the other added more geometry to the room. The coffee table and a side table were positioned to provide places for lamps and setting down drinks.

SOFTEN THE LINES The shag rug went under the coffee table to soften and lighten the floor. The rug doesn't have to cover the entire space. Next, I hid the dark fireplace by putting a large abstract painting (with colors complementing my chosen palette) on the floor in front as a backdrop for the sofa and seating area. To extend the color further across the room, I leaned another smaller, handmade painting up against the wall. A key styling point for this modern look is the placement of the pillows. Pairing round satin and square suede pillows on either side of the sofa yielded a nice play on contrasting textures and shapes, offset by a quirky geometric pillow smack dab in the middle. To keep with the minimalist look the pillows are deliberately placed and showcased more like individual pieces of art, rather than thrown on in a random fashion.

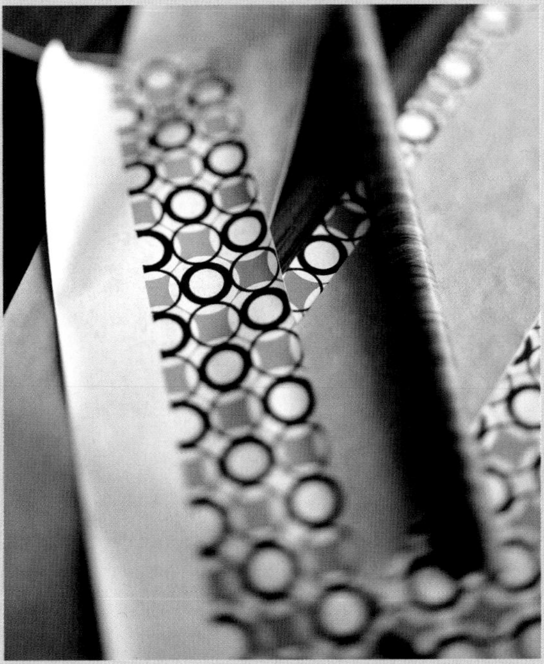

WALLPAPER ART

Create your own art! Even if you don't feel "artistic," you can easily create great works of art with this technique.

Painter's canvas (in any size from an art store)
Wallpaper in various patterns, solids, and textures in your color palette (you'll need enough to cover the canvas)
Small jar of acrylic paint (same color as the wallpaper)
Paintbrush
Scissors
Strong paper glue

- If you are not going to frame the artwork, paint the edge of the canvas approximately 1 inch all around to give it a finished look. Don't worry if the paint gets onto the front of the canvas, as your wallpaper pieces will cover it.
- Cut the wallpaper into strips of different lengths and widths or various geometric shapes and sizes.
- Arrange the wallpaper pieces on the canvas in vertical or horizontal rows—randomly, if using geometric shapes—until you like the result. (If your pieces don't cover the entire canvas, then you'll need to paint the canvas before gluing them down.)
- Glue, let dry, and hang or lean your artwork on the wall!

(See pp. 33 and 34)

PERSONALIZE WITH DETAILS Two Lucite and glass lamps in unusual shapes made a distinct retro statement when placed on either end table; they offered the right mood lighting for a cocktail hour, too. On the mantel, a few white vases peek out from either side of the painting, with just a single stem in one and a single feather in another. Two particularly sculptural vases became objets d'art on the coffee table. In the niches below the table, I set some beautiful books with covers in the color scheme.

8 STYLE THE FOOD AND TABLE As I worked out my modern cocktail party menu, it became clear that even the food should be geometric, and presented in an unfussy way. A large cracker served as a plate, its plain flat expanse contrasting nicely with the plump round olives and the radicchio leaf used as a "bowl" for the goat cheese. I cut the toasts for the asparagus and prosciutto appetizer into sleek rectangular shapes, in keeping with the party's geometric scheme.

TRAY CHIC

Give your imagination free rein when you style food for entertaining. Instead of using the same old serving plates and bowls, look around for interesting flat objects with intriguing colors or textures. An abstract puzzle is used like a place mat under a serving dish. Oversize crackers are stacked to give height and interest to the offering of olives and goat cheese. A classic combination—food and art!

GOAT CHEESE SPREAD IN A RADICCHIO BOWL

1 large radicchio leaf

6 tablespoons chèvre (goat cheese)

2 teaspoons olive oil

Fresh thyme for garnish

1/2 lemon

Carefully rinse and dry radicchio leaf. Place on a serving platter and fill with goat cheese. Using the back of a spoon, press a shallow well in the cheese and drizzle the olive oil in the center. Add a squeeze of lemon and garnish with fresh thyme. Serve with crackers.

SERVES FOUR TO SIX

ASPARAGUS AND PROSCIUTTO TOASTS

9 asparagus spears
6 slices white bread
Freshly shaved Parmesan
9 slices prosciutto—cut in half lengthwise
Salt and pepper to taste

Blanch the asparagus in boiling water for two minutes. Remove from hot water and briefly run under cold water to arrest the cooking process. When cool, cut off the ends of asparagus spears, leaving them approximately 3 inches in length. Slice each spear in half horizontally and set aside.

Toast the bread until lightly golden. Remove crusts and slice each piece of bread into three long sections. Place a few shavings of Parmesan on each slice of toast, and wrap one strip of prosciutto around the toast and cheese. Twist the end of the prosciutto into a rosette. Garnish each toast with an asparagus spear. Add a pinch of salt and freshly ground pepper.

SERVES FOUR TO SIX

DRY MARTINIS

Make martinis two at a time (unless you have a large martini shaker). Your guests won't mind waiting their turn in this time-honored ritual.

1 cup ice cubes
8 ounces gin or vodka
A whisper of vermouth
2 green olives

Chill martini glasses. Fill cocktail shaker with ice and pour in gin or vodka and vermouth. Cover and shake. Drop an olive in each glass and, with an insouciant flourish, pour your martinis, using a strainer.

SERVES TWO

CANDY CANE CHRISTMAS

This easy seasonal makeover is custom-made for a cheery, holiday breakfast.

THE SOUND OF LITTLE FOOTSTEPS DOWN THE HALL, THEN A WHISPER AT YOUR BEDROOM DOOR: "MOM, DAD, SANTA CAME!" Skis and suitcases beckon for an afternoon getaway to the slopes, but the morning belongs to the children, all awake now and scampering around in front of a fire that's just starting to warm the living room. Steam rises from fragrant mugs, Christmas lights glitter against the dark green pine, and the makings of a sumptuous breakfast await your arrival in the kitchen. You're feeling very merry about how little time you spent setting up this magic moment—but best of all is the excitement in the children's eyes at the scene before them. The most precious gifts are the simplest.

magic moment glitter childlike spirit

CANDY CANE CHRISTMAS

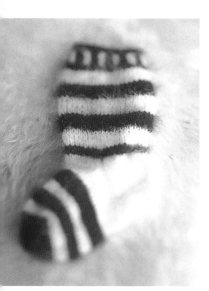

1 WHAT IS THE OCCASION?   A cozy Christmas morning with the family.

2 ENVISION YOUR IDEAL SETTING   A festive yet simple look for the living room that can be created without too much effort or bringing out all the "stuff". This cheerful indoor winter scene delights the children with bright colors and awakens the childlike spirit in grown-ups—perfect for a relaxed breakfast eaten while opening presents.

3 DEVELOP A MAKEOVER STYLE   In the holiday folder of my Style File, I keep a generous collection of Christmas images so my creativity doesn't wear thin in this high-stress season. Looking through the file, I realized that a very simple and childlike setting would strike just the right note, and chose "Candy Cane Christmas" with the kids in mind.

KNIT 'N' STYLE

A hand-knit baby's stocking added a whimsical sense and holiday magic. If you own your own set of knitting needles, this is the perfect opportunity for hands-on styling. A single small stocking can be used as a tree ornament, table accessory, or even tied on to a holiday package.

4 CREATE YOUR STYLE BOARD I began by stretching red velvet ribbon across the top and bottom of my board that I took from my box of Christmas wrapping supplies. Then I pinned up a few red yarn pom poms the kids made at school, a red-and-white-striped napkin, some candy ornaments, a piece of red felt, and several candy canes tied together with a small red bow. I added a few tear sheets from my Christmas Style File—one of red ornaments, another with an adorable image of a child's feet in red and white socks! For a simple but warming menu, I chose a child's perennial favorite—pancakes—but with a special twist.

5 PAINT YOUR COLOR PALETTE I went with the classic peppermint colors—Winter White and Cherry Red.

STYLING SUPPLY LIST

Christmas tree	Christmas stockings
Suede sofa chaise	White candles in various sizes
Beige sofa	Flocked tree branch
White metal table	Artificial cherries
Breakfast tray tables	White and clear glass dishware
Red cotton tablecloth	White and red cotton napkins
Chenille, wool, and faux fur throws	Wrapping paper
Red throw rugs	Ribbon
Throw pillows	Red and white yarn pom-poms
White lights	
Red and white ornaments	
Silver bulb ornaments	
Glass peppermint-candy ornaments	
Glass snowman decantor	

6 GATHER YOUR STYLING SUPPLIES Editing is often the toughest part of styling—especially at Christmastime! To keep from being overwhelmed, take the time to sort and label everything by color palette; gold and silver styling supplies together, for example, whether garland, bulbs, or odd little dishes. Pack silver items with white if you don't have enough of each color to fill a box. You can also organize by style. Your collections of angels can be grouped together and your Santas can all end up together in a different box. Then, if you want to buy some new things you will know exactly what you have in each group, and it will be easier to determine your styling needs. For this makeover, I began by pulling out decorations that were predominantly red and white. Next I went through other closets and drawers in the house and gathered up red and white throws, pillows, tablecloths, and accessories—anything I could get my hands on that fit the candy-cane profile.

7 STYLE THE SPACE **LAY THE FOUNDATION** For this seasonal change, clearing the space means making room for the tree, of course, taking up the area rug, and removing most of the furniture, especially anything dark, in keeping with the tone of the makeover. (If you have dark tables you don't want to remove, cover them with a throw or tablecloth.) I left the two sofas and rearranged the furniture to make the fireplace and mantel the focal point and to allow access to the warmth of our toasty morning fire. The Christmas tree went behind one of the sofas, to be seen without getting in the way. I brought in a long, low white metal table from another room as a coffee table, and added a side table to display the gifts as an alternative to putting them under the tree.

SOFTEN THE LINES I didn't have a red runner the length of the coffee table, so I simply folded a tablecloth lengthwise to create the width I wanted and laid it on the table, leaving some white on each side as a geometric accent. Coordinating the sofas and chaise by covering most of their beige surfaces with red and white blankets and throws unified the seating area and brought a lot of extra warmth. The sofa got a white faux fur and a red wool throw. The chaise received a cozy red chenille afghan as a base, onto which I tossed some red, white, and red-and-white-print pillows. Three red circle rugs (inexpensive enough to buy just for this use) added a note of whimsy, and made handy seats for kids, who inevitably gravitate to the floor to open gifts.

PERFECT POM-POMS

This is a fun project to do with the kids—and you could use some helping hands!

1 cardboard template (directions below)

12 yards plus 12 inches red or white wool yarn for each pom-pom

Scissors

TO MAKE THE TEMPLATE

✿ Determine the size pom-poms you would like to make, and cut a circle of that same size out of a piece of lightweight cardboard. (You may want to use a compass.)

✿ Cut a 1/2-inch circle from the center of the large circle, creating a doughnut shaped template. Here, I've used a 3 1/2-inch template with a 1/2-inch center hole.

TO MAKE THE POM-POM

✿ Take the center of a 12-yard piece of yarn and tie it to the template. Pull yarn so that it is even and ends meet.

✿ Wrap the two strands of yarn through the hole and around the template. Do not wrap it too tight. Continue wrapping in a circular pattern until you've used all of the yarn. (The yarn will wrap approximately two times around.)

✿ With scissors, cut the yarn along the outside edge of the template, carefully gathering it in the center with your hands as you go. Do not drop the yarn or you lose your pom-pom! Tie the 12-inch piece of yarn around the middle of the gathered yarn. Leave the two strands long to use them to hang or tie the pom-pom.

✿ Fluff each pom-pom and hang on the tree or tie onto one of your gifts.

PERSONALIZE WITH DETAILS I wanted to keep the tree decorations very simple so we could enjoy the contrast of the dark green pine against the white walls. First I strung the tree with small all-white lights, then carried through the red-and-white theme in a variety of textures: a red velvet garland, yarn pom-poms (see Style-To, p. 50), red and silver glass bulbs, clear plastic icicles, and, of course, candy canes. On top of the tree, a red velvet bow.

The coffee table was too narrow for a large centerpiece, but I noticed how pretty it looked when we set ornaments on it at random while decorating the tree. It often pays off to follow up on these little surprises you get while styling, and I capitalized on this one by scattering a few ornaments, gifts, and decorative items down the runner, as if the Santa's elves had been interrupted in their preparations.

The flocked tree-branch mantel display (see Style-To, below) became an elegant white-on-white display, and at night the surrounding candles created a glowing spotlight on the glittering branch, delighting the children with its fairy-tale effect.

Finally, I wrapped all the gifts in coordinating red-and-white papers and ribbons so their festive presence became part of the decor.

8 STYLE THE FOOD AND TABLE   Using separate breakfast trays is a practical idea—it prevents the kids from dripping maple syrup on the coffee table, and once everyone is finished with breakfast, it can be easily cleared away without interrupting the main event—presents! I used a red-trimmed white place mat to line each tray, and the pancakes looked delicious served on a clear glass plate with a white dish underneath and candy canes on the side.

WINTER CHERRY MANTEL DISPLAY

1 tree branch, sized to fit your mantel

2 cans white spray paint

1 can spray adhesive

1 bag fine flocking snow (from a craft store)

A dozen or so pairs of artificial cherries connected at the top

Museum wax (available at most craft or hardware stores)

❈ This project should be done outdoors

❈ Cover the work surface with newspaper or plastic and place the branch on top.

❈ Spray paint the front and back of the branch white and allow it to dry.

❈ Spray adhesive on the branch a section at a time and sprinkle with snow immediately. Continue this process until the entire branch is covered. (You only need to flock the side that will be visible.)

❈ Hang the artificial cherries randomly among the branches.

❈ To secure the branch on the mantel, you can use museum wax or a large piece of clay to hold the base of the branch while it's leaning against the wall. The wax will keep the base from slipping off the mantel and is removable.

Note: You may need to trim the back branches and the base if they are not flat so that the branch leans easily against the wall.

(See p. 45)

CINNAMON COFFEE
AND COCOA

Place a fresh cinnamon stick in each cup. Pour in your coffee or cocoa and allow to infuse for a minute or so, then serve.

RICOTTA PANCAKES WITH
HONEYCOMB AND BANANAS

1 cup flour

2 teaspoons baking powder

2 teaspoons ground ginger

2 tablespoons granulated sugar

1 cup flaked coconut

4 eggs, separated

1 1/4 cups milk

15 ounces ricotta cheese

2 bananas, sliced on an angle

Fresh honeycomb for garnish (optional)

Maple syrup

Mix the flour, baking powder, ginger, and sugar in a bowl. Add in the coconut.

In a separate bowl, combine the egg yolks, milk, and three-quarters of the ricotta (reserving the rest for later). Add mixture to dry ingredients and mix until blended.

Using an electric mixer, beat the egg whites until soft peaks form. Fold into the batter.

Lightly coat bottom of frying pan or griddle with nonstick cooking spray or butter. (A mini frying pan or a blini pan is perfect for small pancakes.) Pour 1/3 cup of batter in hot pan and cook over low heat until bubbles form on the surface. Flip and cook until golden.

To serve, stack three or more on each plate; add a dollop of ricotta, several slices of banana, and maple syrup. (Pancakes can be kept warm in oven while the remainder of the batter is prepared.) Garnish with a candy cane or fresh honeycomb.

SERVES FOUR

cinnamon stick **sweet tooth** maple syrup

VINTAGE ROMANCE

This one's for the girls: a special-occasion room transformation that unabashedly piles on the lace and flowers.

ANY WEDDING IS THE GRAND OPENING TO A BEAUTIFUL LOVE STORY, AND EVERYONE HAS A PART TO PERFORM. When you throw a bridal shower, think like a movie art director. Imagine the bride as a leading lady who deserves a set that makes her feel like a star. Treat your styling supplies as stage props and go all out expressing your theatrical flair. Play around with jewelry, shoes, dresses, hats, beaded bags, and antique vases—anything that whispers "romantic"—to create a feminine space. Serve small, delicious bites, little indulgences that don't threaten to strain the seams of anyone's party dress. And don't forget to lavish her with masses of flowers; what woman (or movie set) ever had too many?

antique touches little indulgences romantic ambience

VINTAGE ROMANCE

ROMANTIC FLORALS

The right flowers are very important to setting the mood for this makeover.

✿ Choose dainty, lacy, feminine cottage-garden flowers, like hydrangeas and roses, in your color palette.

✿ Use a variety of vases in different sizes and shapes, mixing and matching at will.

✿ Place single vases in some spots and group three small vases in others.

✿ Try adding fresh fruits to your arrangements. Filling the bottom of a clear glass vase with lemons or limes or tiny apples is a nice touch.

1   WHAT IS THE OCCASION?   An afternoon bridal shower with close friends and family.

2   ENVISION YOUR IDEAL SETTING   A feminine, romantic living room where the girls feel they're just hanging out in the bedroom chatting. They can curl up on the sofa or on cushions on the floor. The makeover should have the feeling of a backstage dressing room on opening night—lots of flowers, the congratulations flowing like wine.

3   DEVELOP A MAKEOVER STYLE   As I began to look through my Style File for romantic images, I was immediately drawn to turn-of-the-century fashions: lace and ruffles, old-fashioned parasols, Edwardian hats, Victorian lockets, and high-button shoes. Clearly the style had to be "Vintage Romance."

4 CREATE YOUR STYLE BOARD Keeping romance in mind, I began with a piece of lace, which I pinned up alongside some pictures of lush, full-blown roses and hydrangeas. I added a magazine ad depicting a lipstick the same shade of blushing pink as one of the roses. I then twined some pieces of ribbon that matched the bedroom pillows through a strand of fake pearls and draped it on the board. Swatches of pale organza and soft mauve velvet framed a romantic poem to keep me in the mood. When I found a picture of a salad with edible flowers, the lightbulb flashed—"Ah, we can *eat* the flowers, too"—and on the board it went.

STYLING SUPPLY LIST

Antique wood chaise

Suede sofa chaise

Black coffee table

Antique vanity

Hand-painted fireplace screen

Vintage gold-and-pink rug

Pink matelasse bedcover, pink organza

Decorative pillows in pink, gold, cream, and floral prints

Gold brocade tablecloth

Antique lamps and beaded hanging lamps

Wrought-iron candelabra with crystal drops

Miscellaneous silver and glass vases

Vintage dress form

Vintage dresses, apron, shawls, scarves, petticoats, blouse

Vintage hat and small beaded handbag

Small beaded jewelry box, pearls, and antique jewelry

Gold-leafed frame

Mismatched china plates with floral designs and gilt

Vintage mirror tray and perfume bottles

Simple wineglasses and silver flatware

Antique doll

Feathers

Fresh flowers—hydrangeas, roses, and so on

5 PAINT YOUR COLOR PALETTE Antique Gold, Blushing Pink, Soft Mauve, Petticoat White, and a hint of Hydrangea Green rounded out my palette. For this makeover, it may be a good idea to briefly skip to Step 6 and pull a few styling supplies so that you can see what you have to work with. Choose your foundation colors by reviewing the available throws, rugs, bedcovers, tablecloths and other large pieces of fabric.

6 GATHER YOUR STYLING SUPPLIES If the opportunity exists, rummage through an attic filled with Grandma's gowns and shawls—or at least scour the closet for any vintage clothes you've collected, then see what you can beg, borrow, or steal from your funkier friends. You can also take a trip to a nearby thrift store and pick up an old vintage hat or two. In addition to all the old-fashioned petticoats, blouses, shawls, hats, and fashion accessories you can find, be on the lookout for dressing table or boudoir items such as perfume bottles, jewelry boxes, vanity trays,

TEXTURE satin and lace vintage touches antique jewelry

and so on. Collect china plates in several different pretty floral patterns. If it's the right season, call around and ask permission to pick roses from friends and neighbors' gardens; otherwise, be sure to pick up your flowers a day or two ahead of time so they are in full bloom for the special day.

7 STYLE THE SPACE   **LAY THE FOUNDATION** The living room had a suede chaise and a sofa that together seemed too heavy, so I said good-bye to the sofa. The chaise, however, was so perfect—feminine, delicate, and open at one end—that I brought in another one, this one in antique wood. To enhance the theatrical dressing room effect, I also brought in a vanity (not normally seen in the living room), which would provide a perfect spot for my array of perfume bottles and vintage collections. Though my brown wooden table didn't fit my color palette, it was all I had, so I kept it and planned to cover it up during the styling process. I arranged the furniture in a radial pattern around the coffee table to create an intimate gathering area, and brought in a screen to cover the dark, unused fireplace and close up the space. The screen I had was not as big as I would have liked, but so what! Better than a dark hole.

COUTURE SCULPTURE

Dress form or mannequin (you can purchase or rent one from a prop house or display store)

Vintage clothing, lace pieces, or an antique wedding dress

Vintage jewelry, including brooches and hatpins

Fresh flowers

Straight or safety pins

✿ Begin by partly dressing the form with a piece of clothing or lace (I layered two skirts and pinned them in back).

✿ Gracefully drape one or more other pieces (I used another skirt to make the "blouse" and added a lace shawl), securing with pins.

✿ Hang and pin jewelry; festoon with flowers.

ROMANTIC VIGNETTE

This romantic vignette is created by grouping three items together with the largest one in the back. These should be various textures, sizes, and shapes.

SOFTEN THE LINES I started by putting the Victorian rug under the coffee table to warm up the floor, which would serve as a seating area. The coffee table posed no problem once I found a pink matelasse bedcover to drape on top. Once you've put a bedspread on the table, why not a tablecloth on the chaise? This gold brocade blended beautifully with the suede. I threw a beaded shawl on the back of the second chaise; one more mixed medium to add softness and warmth. Next, I draped and placed the dress form (see Style-To, p. 63) to capture the mood of the makeover and add to the theatrical feel. A framed antique blouse (see Style-To, below) hung above the fireplace, and a generous toss of pillows onto the chaises finished this styling phase.

PERSONALIZE WITH DETAILS Since this makeover calls for an abundance of small touches, don't try to figure them out in advance; just gather your items and go! Make groupings and then move things around until your artist's eye approves. I started by placing several antique lamps before creating arrangements on the mantle, vanity, and coffee table. Invent little groupings or vignettes with dishes, vases, jewelry, hats, silverware, and other items, as if staging a movie's drawing-room scene. Instead of simply putting the jewelry box on the end table, group it with a vase and some antique jewelry. You'll find an arrangement often seems to tell a story, as you imagine a romantic heroine setting down a beaded purse next to a vase of roses, or removing her hat before reading a love letter. Last but not least, add plenty of cut flowers. Hydrangeas and roses brought sweet perfume and filled the room with romance.

8 STYLE THE FOOD AND TABLE   The romantic style cried out for flowers in the food as well as on the table, so I used edible pansies as colorful ingredients in the salad, prettied up the tartlets with hydrangeas (*not* edible, take note!), and served the wine spritzers on a mirrored tray scattered with petals. Beautiful pieces of vintage floral china and porcelain, no two the same because they'd been collected one by one, are perfect for serving up your guests a little bit of romance.

PRETTY AS A PICTURE

Antique gold-leafed frame

Hammer and nail

Vintage wardrobe items—silk jacket, embroidered blouse, and so on

Delicate or satin clothes hanger

⚜ Place a small nail along the top, back center of the frame to attach the clothes hanger.

⚜ Place the frame on the mantel or sideboard and lean it against the wall.

⚜ Hold up the items you're considering. Try a few different variations to see what looks best in the room before placing your final choice on the hanger. (See p. 57)

INDIVIDUAL SAVORY TARTLETS

6 four-inch quiche pans

2 sheets of premade puff pastry crust (available in supermarket freezers)

1/2 small white onion, finely chopped

1/4 cup leek, finely chopped (white and green parts only)

1 tablespoon butter

2 eggs

1 cup heavy whipping cream

1/4 cup chives, finely chopped

4 strips of bacon, lightly fried and chopped

3 small tomatoes, sliced

1/4 teaspoon salt

1/4 teaspoon freshly ground pepper

Preheat oven to 375°. Lightly mist the quiche pans with cooking spray. Lay each sheet of pastry on a floured surface. (Pastry sheet may need to be rolled out slightly to have enough dough for all 6 quiche pans.) Cut each sheet of pastry into four equal squares and lay one square into each pan, pressing down gently to fit. Trim any extra dough from edges.

Melt butter in sauté pan, and add onions and leeks. Sauté until transparent, about 5 to 7 minutes. Remove from heat.

In a medium bowl, whisk together the eggs and cream. Add the cooked onion, leek, bacon, and chives and stir thoroughly. Mix in salt and pepper.

Fill each pastry shell approximately three-quarters full and place one slice of tomato in the center of each tartlet. Bake for 15 to 20 minutes, or until the tartlet is slightly firm to the touch and crust is golden brown. Let tartlets cool for several minutes before removing from pans. Place each tartlet on an individual plate and garnish with fresh flowers.

SERVES SIX

PINOT NOIR SPRITZERS

1 bottle pinot noir (can substitute other red wine)

1 cup freshly squeezed orange juice

16 ounces soda water

1 teaspoon sweetened or fresh lime juice

1 orange, sliced into thin half-moons

In a pitcher or punch bowl, combine all ingredients, except orange slices. Chill before serving. Serve in wine glasses garnished with a slice of orange and an edible flower.

SERVES SIX

MIXED GREENS SALAD WITH EDIBLE FLOWERS AND RASPBERRY VINAIGRETTE

Vinaigrette

1/4 cup raspberry vinegar

1/4 cup cranberry juice

3 tablespoons olive oil

1 1/2 tablespoons honey

1 teaspoon sugar

2 teaspoons orange zest

1 teaspoon salt

1/2 teaspoon freshly ground pepper

In a small bowl, mix together above ingredients with a wire whisk or fork. Set aside.

Salad

6 cups mixed field greens (watercress, radicchio, arugula, butter lettuce, etc.)

1 bunch radishes, whole

1/2 cup dried cranberries

1/4 cup pine nuts

1 cup edible flowers (rose petals, nasturtiums, or pansies)

Place the greens, radishes, cranberries and pine nuts in a large mixing bowl. Pour the dressing over the greens and toss. Add salt and pepper to taste. Transfer to a serving plate and garnish with flowers. (Option: Top with goat cheese.)

SERVES SIX

THE DINING

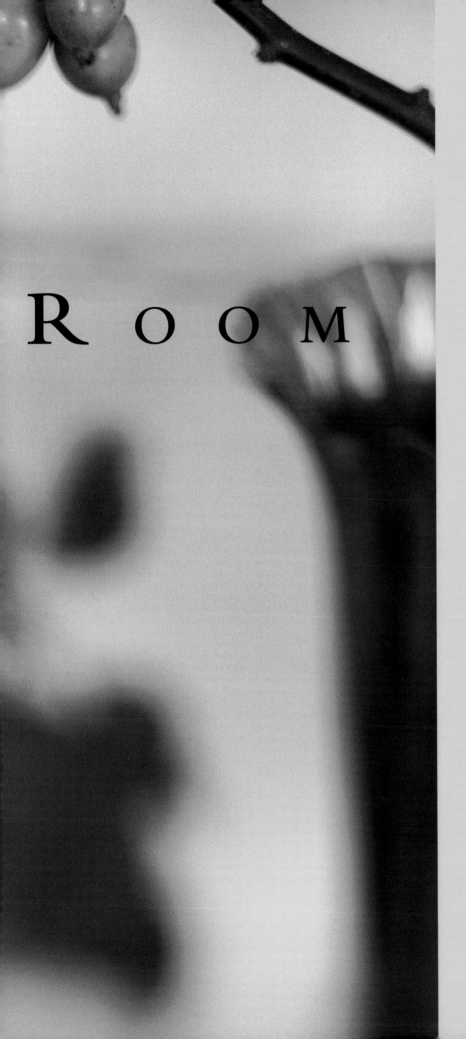

R O O M

CHAPTER 3

*Best known as a place for
formal sit-down dinners, the dining
room is much more versatile than you
might realize. Styling can transform this
space into a cheerful spot for casual
spontaneous meals, a seasonal setting
for a Thanksgiving gathering,
or a festive site for a fun
birthday bash.*

ITALIAN TRATTORIA

THANKSGIVING FEAST

ASIAN FUSION

Some of the best parties are spontaneous, but it takes confidence to say, "Please stay for dinner!" My "Italian Trattoria" casual makeover creates a comfortable, enjoyable space that's easy to dress up at a moment's notice. The simple white-on-white foundation and Mediterranean-inspired accents like olive branches, lemons, and sisal add up to a neighborhood trattoria look that's contemporary but warm and versatile. ❖ The seasonal makeover, "Thanksgiving Feast," takes a lavish hand with the classics: an inviting, bountiful table and warm fall colors. The patina of beautiful handed-down objects blends with rustic harvest elements to create intimate elegance and an homage to Mother Earth. ❖ A party is always an excuse to push your creative bounds and discover just how different your dining room can be. My special occasion "Asian Fusion" makeover offers proof that a little inventive shopping for inexpensive styling supplies can sometimes bring a more dramatic change than big-deal purchases. Here, an array of Asian-inspired objects transports the dining room as fast as you unpack your shopping bags—styling at the speed of take-out.

ITALIAN TRATTORIA

This white-on-white dining room offers guests a warm, casual welcome like your favorite neighborhood restaurant.

YOU KNOW THAT FAVORITE NEIGHBORHOOD SPOT—the place where you pop in for a bite after a long day, and the owner knows your name. You love to meet friends here because it's just like home but without the stuffy formal-dining-room feel. This wise host lures you in by offering a light and airy setting where the feeling of the outdoors is always present and the pasta primavera is as fresh as the atmosphere. In this scenario, that wise host is you!

When you create a home trattoria that's ready for supper at the drop of a hat, your dining room will quickly become a favorite family hangout, an inviting spot for spur-of-the-moment meals with friends, or the perfect venue for romantic late-night bites. Think Mediterranean thoughts—white curtains billowing on sea breezes, lemon and olive trees, sun-bleached wood, steaming cappuccino, and a welcome respite from the pressures of the outside world. Sure, your local trattoria may see you less, but now just-like-home is home!

favorite and familiar inviting trattoria style

1 WHAT IS THE OCCASION? Easy everyday meals with family or friends.

2 ENVISION YOUR IDEAL SETTING A clean, casual dining room with a setup that is simple and unfussy. It should always be ready for spontaneous sit-down dinners, but still informal enough for casual meals.

3 DEVELOP A MAKEOVER STYLE With casual in mind, I immediately thought of one of my favorite restaurants. I pictured: white dishes, breadboards, oil cruets and fresh lemons. This style screamed "Italian Trattoria," the place where you feel welcome, laugh, and eat pasta!

TEA TOWEL TABLECLOTH

If you have a sewing machine, you can finish this project in a snap—or pop over to see a friend who sews.

Cotton tea towels or napkins
Thread in a coordinating color
Sewing machine

❖ Measure your table, adding one foot on all sides for overhang. Take the dimensions with you (and a measuring tape) when you purchase the tea towels, so you can determine the number of towels you need.

❖ Pick a simple cotton towel in your color scheme.

❖ Before you begin sewing, lay out all your towels and play with the design. If the towels have stripes on them, you don't have to line them all up perfectly; only the edges have to align.

❖ Sew the towels together like a large quilt.

4 CREATE YOUR STYLE BOARD   I have a beautiful olive tree outside my kitchen window, and I love the way its branches drape artfully down to the ground. On my windowsill, I always keep a bowl of fresh lemons from my tree. As I gazed at the combination of the olive branches and yellow lemons, it seemed fresh and light. The branch pinned to my board, I went to my herb garden and cut a sprig of rosemary, its silvery green a picturesque partner to the olive branch, and its piney aroma jump-starting ideas for a meal of fresh, intense flavors. Up went a natural linen napkin and some daisies tied with a piece of raffia—and then, hungry already, I started searching for simple pasta recipes.

STYLING SUPPLY LIST

Dining table

Wooden chairs

Sideboard

Sisal rug

Tea towels

Artwork for the walls

Miscellaneous assorted white dishware

Simple flatware

Sturdy glassware

Linen napkins

Yellow ribbon and rings

Breadboard

Vase with daisy

Lemons and lemon leaves

Olive branch

Bread sticks. cookies and dried pasta

Glass canisters

SIMPLE GREENS

A simple green leaf salad with olive oil and balsamic vinegar is a perfect accompaniment for this quick dinner set-up.

lemon yellow **daisy white** natural linen

5 PAINT YOUR COLOR PALETTE   Lemon Yellow, Daisy White, Natural Linen, and Olive Green—this scheme needed no improvement.

6 GATHER YOUR STYLING SUPPLIES   Everyone should own a set of inexpensive white dishware. Like a simple black dress that you can dress up or down depending on the occasion, white dishes can be styled however you like and are a good investment in your creative future. Restaurants rely on white linens because they're easy to bleach and clean, and white plates because they complement the colors of your food. Other trattoria styling supplies include cruets of olive oil and vinegar, bread, lemons, dried pasta, and bowls of fresh tomatoes picked from the garden. Keep an eye out for natural textures that contrast with the smooth white dishes: a wooden breadboard, crusty loaves of bread, a sisal rug. Herbs can be used in many ways in this makeover, so I recommend perching a few pots on a windowsill, or placing mixed cut herbs in a small glass vase on the sideboard.

7 STYLE THE SPACE   **LAY THE FOUNDATION** This makeover requires stripping down the dining room to its bare essentials—so pack up those heavy curtains or drapes, anything with prints or patterns, knickknacks, and any furniture besides a table, chairs, and a sideboard. The simplest possible furniture arrangement focuses all attention on the dining table, the center of activity. If possible you want to avoid looming china cabinets and side tables, which can seem too weighty or busy.

RIBBON NAPKIN RING

Ribbon (one foot per place setting)

3/4-inch metal rings (one per ribbon)

Needle and thread

Napkins

❖ Wrap the end of the ribbon around the ring and fasten with a few stitches.

❖ Iron and fold your napkins.

❖ Wrap the ribbon around the napkin once and tie off around the ring.

SOFTEN THE LINES To bring the outdoors in and to keep the room fresh and light, I left the center window, which faces a private garden, unadorned. Sheers on the side windows cut down on glare without diminishing light. Next, a sisal rug warms the floor underfoot with a natural earth tone that doesn't mind bread crumbs. An olive branch over the table creates an indoor canopy reminiscent of a tree's shady arms. Finally, I whipped up a tablecloth out of tea towels (see Style-To, p. 74). Inexpensive, easy to find, and a snap to wash and iron, tea towels are always a great styling tool, and here they appear in an unexpected role.

PERSONALIZE WITH DETAILS My inspiration for finding a pretty everyday display that could stay in place for guests was back at my local trattoria, where the sideboards were filled with white serving dishes, bowls, teapots, extra glassware, breadsticks, and dried pasta, all right at hand with no running back and forth to the kitchen. (I had a similar setup in my restaurants, and boy, is it handy!) Why not do the same at home? A simple centerpiece kept the table uncluttered: a humble breadboard topped with handsome artisan bread next to a vase of daisies.

8 STYLE THE FOOD AND TABLE Set each place with a charger, bowl, and napkin (see Style-To, p. 79), and a water glass with a fresh slice of lemon. Dishes of oil and vinegar on the breadboard are ready for dunking, just as you'd find in a restaurant. In keeping with the trattoria style, add herbs at will—as garnish on the food, attached to a napkin ring, or displayed in a vase. Serving the Tomato, Bocconcini, and Basil Salad in individual portions plated in the kitchen adds a sophisticated touch to the meal. The spaghetti with peas and prosciutto should also be dished into single portions, restaurant style. For added flair, twist pasta into high peaks and garnish individually.

SPAGHETTI WITH PEAS AND PROSCIUTTO

1 pound dried spaghetti

1 cup fresh or frozen peas

3 tablespoons olive oil

2 cloves garlic, minced

4 ounces sliced prosciutto, torn into small strips

Shaved Parmesan to taste

Sea salt and ground pepper to taste

Cook spaghetti just a few minutes less than package instructions until al dente. (You may add one tablespoon of olive oil and one tablespoon of salt to boiling water, if desired.) Drain and lightly rinse with cold water. Set aside.

Cook the peas in boiling water for 2 or 3 minutes, or just until tender.

In a large frying pan, heat the olive oil, add the minced garlic, and cook on medium heat for several minutes, being careful not to burn. Add the prosciutto and lightly pan fry for another several minutes. Remove a few pieces of prosciutto from the pan and set aside. They will later be used for garnish. Reduce heat to low, add the cooked pasta and peas, and season with sea salt and freshly ground pepper. Heat thoroughly and toss to combine.

Remove from heat and serve on individual plates, twisting the pasta in a circular motion to create a peak. Garnish with a piece of prosciutto and several shavings of Parmesan. Add salt and pepper to taste.

SERVES FOUR

TOMATO, BOCCONCINI, AND BASIL SALAD

This can be made a few hours in advance and kept in the refrigerator, but be sure to bring out an hour before serving, as tomatoes are much more flavorful at room temperature.

4 Roma tomatoes, sliced lengthwise (discard end pieces)
4 small bocconcini (a form of mozzarella), sliced
1/2 cup fresh basil
3 tablespoons olive oil
Coarse sea salt and freshly ground black pepper

Layer tomatoes and bocconcini on a platter and top with fresh basil. Drizzle with olive oil and add salt and pepper to taste. Serve with crispy Italian bread.

SERVES FOUR

PLATE PRESENTATION

For an artful presentation, create individual servings by placing a slice of tomato, then a slice of cheese, and a fresh basil leaf on each plate. Using a spoon, carefully drop olive oil around the tomato.

ROAST TURKEY AND CHESTNUT STUFFING
SWEET POTATO FRIES
PEAS AND ROASTED BABY ONIONS
BUTTERMILK ROLLS
ORANGE CRANBERRY RELISH
APPLE, PUMPKIN AND PECAN PIES

THANKSGIVING FEAST

This seasonal dining room makeover teams elegance and earthiness to celebrate the harvest in style.

THANKSGIVING ISN'T LIKE OTHER CELEBRATIONS. This is the day you break out all the heirlooms and then some, for how are you going to serve all these people, all this food? In all the excitement, the rules of tradition converge with your contemporary creative spirit. Platters that show traces of previous generations are heaped with crops fresh from the farm, and you dig into rustic dishes with Grandmother's best silverware.

This is the time to celebrate today's bounty alongside elegant treasures from the past. By honoring the earth and elevating the occasion with sophisticated touches, you knit together the past and future with hope for continued good fortune. A toast then, to a Thanksgiving feast!

traditional feasting **heirloom** bountiful celebration

1 WHAT IS THE OCCASION?   The autumn season and its signature holiday, Thanksgiving.

2 ENVISION YOUR IDEAL SETTING   Warm, cozy, rich with fall colors—a generously festive but not too formal dining room buffet. A feeling of history, yet with plenty of fresh, stylish contemporary touches to set this year's celebration apart from last year's and focus the glow on the moment. Like family and the seasons themselves, the surroundings should be familiar but charged with the possibilities of change.

3 DEVELOP A MAKEOVER STYLE   Thanksgiving suggests the opulence of a feast and the simplicity of harvest foods. It was simple: "Thanksgiving Feast."

GILDED FRUIT AND VEGETABLES

Bring a baroque touch to the table with your own harvest still life.

Gold gilding paint (from an art store)

Paintbrush (half-inch)

Assorted fruits and vegetables (artichokes, winter squash, pears, pomegranates, grapes)

Plastic gloves

❖ Wash and thoroughly dry the fruit and vegetables.

❖ Paint each piece of fruit and vegetable with gold paint, covering some completely, lightly brushing others so that most of the original color shows through and leaving some unpainted except for a few highlights of gold.

❖ Allow to dry, then arrange in a pedestal bowl.

Note: As lovely as these look, they are not suitable for consumption.

4 CREATE YOUR STYLE BOARD First, I pulled all the pictures of Thanksgiving dinners from my holiday Style File for some fresh ideas for the menu and tacked them on the board. Leaning an antique still-life painting next to the Style Board seemed to help set the warm autumn tone I desired. I looked around for possible tablecloth fabrics and pulled a piece of burlap from my stash that had the humble quality I was looking for. Set against the elegant silver I planned to use, the burlap would have just the right contrast. I hung an old silver napkin ring on a pushpin alongside the burlap. Perfect.

STYLING SUPPLY LIST

Dining table

Sofa table

Chair

Cream matelasse bedcover

Painter's cloth, burlap, and a linen runner

Old tapestry drape

Assorted white dishes and serving plates

Silver plates, chargers, vases, flatware, candlesticks

Dark metal lamp, pedestal bowl, and antique clock

Leather-bound books

Paintings of fruit and/or vegetables with rich, aged tones

Branches, seedpods, etc.

Glass decanters

Assorted fruit and vegetables, to be gilded

5 PAINT YOUR COLOR PALETTE Russet Brown, Harvest Moon Gold, Warm Caramel, Divinity Cream, and Antiqued Silver were the shades for my autumnal mix.

6 GATHER YOUR STYLING SUPPLIES The best way to begin a seasonal styling project is to decide on the dishes and silverware and then pull out all possible platters, breadboards, serving tureens, even the silver tray from your coffee or tea set. Try a few preliminary groupings to see what works together. After you look over your best-loved family treasures (I also picked out an antique clock, a dark metal pedestal bowl, books, and paintings), survey the house for fabrics, tablecloths, bedcovers, or throws—look for fall colors and textures like burnt sienna, deep oranges, burlap, linen, tapestries, rich browns, and so on. Next, take a walk in the crisp autumn air and gather from the bounty outdoors: colored leaves, bright berries, seedpods, branches, dried grasses, and so on.

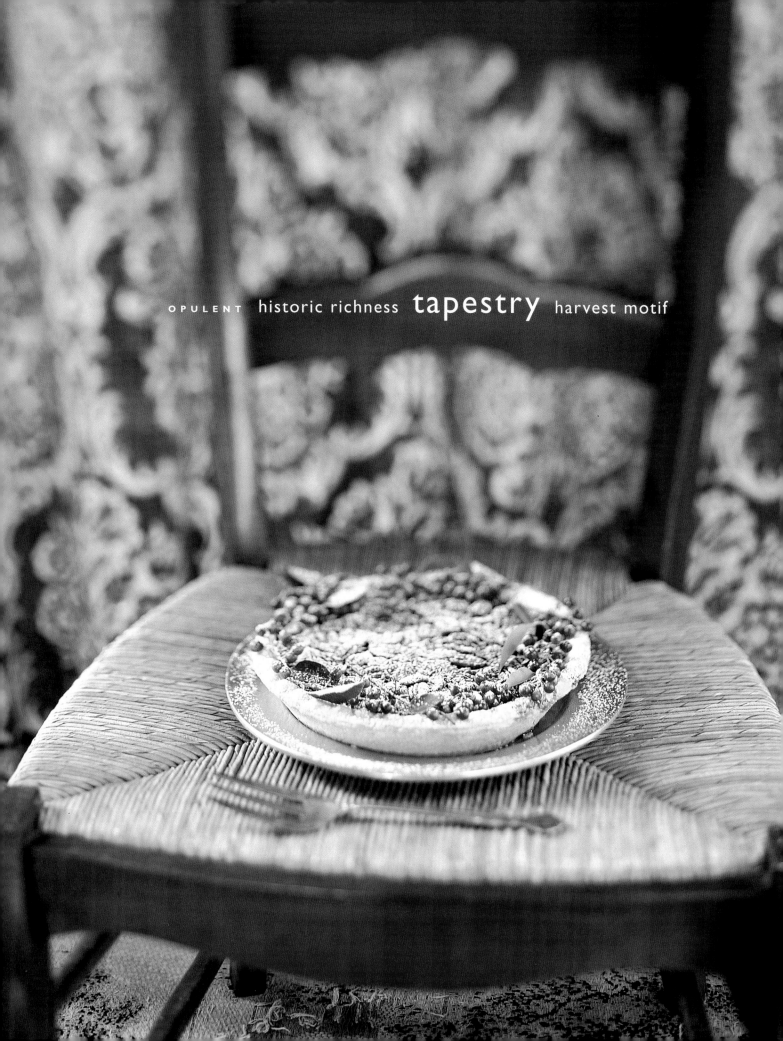

OPULENT historic richness **tapestry** harvest motif

7 STYLE THE SPACE **LAY THE FOUNDATION** Since there was going to be plenty of food, I left the dining table, which would serve as a buffet, in the center of the room so guests could flow around it. Using some furniture from other parts of the house is a fun seasonal change, so I positioned a sofa table to act as a sideboard and a small occasional table to fill a bare space next to the window.

SOFTEN THE LINES My soft styling supplies were a study in contrast, some delicate (like the gauze curtains), some rustic (like the burlap table cover). A rug in my palette's brown, cream, and caramel colors warmed up the floor. Because it's so hard to find really large tablecloths, I used a painter's drop cloth as the first layer, allowing it to billow slightly at the bottom. For more texture, I added a cream-colored textured bedcover and then a rough-edged piece of burlap (that I had left over from a Halloween project), finishing it off with a natural linen runner. I hung a single panel of a tapestry curtain (since I only had one) in rich golds and browns in the middle of the three windows and added cream-colored gauze fabric on either side to balance the tapestry's opulent weight and to soften the light coming through the windows. After draping a deep gold patterned fabric over the small table, I bunched it under at the bottom to finish it off. Next I played curator with some still-life paintings of harvest motifs, propping two up against the wall on the sideboard so they'd be easy to change later, then hanging a third alongside (I made sure the tops of all three were aligned). I set a fourth small painting down for a moment on the adjacent chair while figuring out where to put it, and it looked so cute that I left it!

PERSONALIZE WITH DETAILS I find it best to place the tallest elements first—in this case, a silver vase filled with apple branches on one end of the sideboard. Next to the apple branch vase I placed wine-filled glass decanters on a silver tray. An antique metal clock sat slightly off center with a bowl of fresh fruit.

    For the round table near the window, I brought in a lamp with a dark metal base and a leaf-patterned parchment shade, adding a stack of worn books with leather covers for an aura of richness and history and a sense that this room was for more than just dining. The extra table vignette gave a more lived-in feeling.

8 STYLE THE FOOD AND TABLE A bowl of gilded fruits and vegetables (see Style-To, p. 86) became the centerpiece on the main table. This was so easy to do and inexpensive, as well! I set out white stoneware dishes, but fine china would work, too. Presentation is very important on a buffet table, so have your food styling supplies handy and ready to garnish: long branches of rosemary for the turkey, stems of fresh mint for the peas and onions, whole leaves of sage for the dressing. You can make store-bought pies look homemade by sprinkling them with some powdered sugar and styling the top with fruits and small leaves.

SUGARED GRAPES

Here's another beautiful way to embellish harvest fruits for a stylish accent on a plate.

1 bunch of grapes, rinsed and dried

1 pasteurized egg white

2 tablespoons water

3 tablespoons granulated sugar

Cooling rack

❖ Place the grapes on a cooling rack.

❖ Combine egg white and water, whisking briefly until thoroughly blended but not foamy, to make the egg wash.

❖ Brush the egg wash over the bunch of grapes, avoiding any foam that may have formed.

❖ Sprinkle granulated sugar over grapes, turning the bunch gently to get any hard-to-reach areas. Coverage doesn't need to be perfect, as variations in the sugar add to the look.

Note: If these grapes are for consumption, make sure to use pasteurized egg whites, found in most supermarkets.

ROAST TURKEY

Over the years I've found the best way to cook a turkey is to cover it with cheesecloth. This makes it crispy on top while still keeping it moist inside.

1 14-to-16 lb. turkey

Salt

6 cloves garlic, pressed

1 tablespoon poultry seasoning

1 large cheesecloth

1 cup butter, melted

Chestnut stuffing, cooled (see recipe below)

Preheat the oven to 450°. Place the turkey in a roasting pan, and rub with salt and pressed garlic. Sprinkle with poultry seasoning. Spoon the cooled stuffing into the turkey just before roasting. Close the cavity with small skewers and a crisscrossed string or sew with a large needle. Fasten the drumsticks together with string, as well.

Saturate the cheesecloth with melted butter, lay it over the turkey, and tuck around the legs and cavity to completely cover. Place turkey in the oven and reduce heat to 350°. Roast for approximately 20 minutes per pound (or according to turkey's cooking instructions).

While roasting, baste the turkey with its drippings, using a turkey baster, every 30 minutes. When turkey is finished, remove from the oven and immediately peel off the cheesecloth. Allow the turkey to cool before carving.

SERVES TWELVE

CHESTNUT STUFFING

1/4 cup butter

1 small onion, chopped

1 stalk of celery, chopped

1 teaspoon dried sage

1 teaspoon dried tarragon

1 teaspoon dried thyme

1/2 teaspoon salt

2 tablespoons fresh parsley

5 cups bread crumbs

1 1/2 cups chestnuts

Up to 1/4 cup vegetable or chicken broth

Freshly ground pepper to taste

Melt the butter in a small pan. Add the onion and celery and sauté until transparent. Set aside.

Combine the dry ingredients in a large bowl. Add the cooked onion and celery and just enough broth to barely moisten the bread crumbs. Mix gently until combined.

Cool and spoon into the turkey cavity. Extra stuffing can be cooked separately in a greased baking dish.

SERVES SIX

SWEET POTATO FRIES

4 tablespoons brown sugar

1 1/2 teaspoons nutmeg

1 teaspoon cinnamon

1/4 teaspoon cloves

1/2 teaspoon salt

2 cups vegetable oil

6 medium sweet potatoes, peeled and cut lengthwise
into 1-inch strips

2 tablespoons butter, melted

In a small bowl, combine brown sugar, nutmeg, cinnamon, cloves, and salt. Set aside.

Heat oil on medium high heat in a deep skillet. When oil is hot, carefully add the sweet potatoes using tongs. Make sure potatoes are completely covered by the oil. (You may need to cook these in several batches depending on the size of your skillet.) Deep-fry the sweet potatoes until golden brown, about 8 to 10 minutes.

Drain the fries on paper towels and transfer to a shallow dish. Drizzle with melted butter and sugar mixture and toss gently to coat. Transfer to serving dish and serve immediately.

SERVES SIX

PEAS AND ROASTED BABY ONIONS

1 lb pearl onions, peeled

1 tablespoon olive oil

3 cups fresh or frozen peas

Salt and freshly ground pepper to taste

Fresh mint sprigs for garnish

Preheat the oven to 350°. Place the onions on a baking sheet and coat with olive oil. Roast until golden, approximately 30 minutes.

While the onions are roasting, cook the peas in boiling water for 5 minutes. Do not overcook. Remove from water immediately and combine with the roasted onions in a serving bowl.

Top with a dab of butter and salt and pepper to taste. Garnish with fresh mint.

SERVES SIX

MENU
VIETNAMESE-STYLE SPRING ROLLS WITH DIPPING SAUCE
YOUR FAVORITE ASIAN TAKE-OUT
STEAMED RICE
ASIAN SODAS AND GREEN TEA ICE CREAM
FORTUNE COOKIES AND HOT JASMINE TEA

ASIAN FUSION

This festive setting turns take-out into a quick stylish party.

IMAGINE HURRYING INTO AN EMPTY DINING ROOM—EVEN A CON-
FERENCE ROOM—AND UNPACKING A PARTY! Like a paper lantern unfolding,
colors and shapes pop out, place settings fall into eye-catching configurations, boxes of
steaming food release an ineffable swirl of fragrance into the air. Your guests walk in and are instantly
wowed by this colorful, abundant space, which was only moments ago a plain, lifeless room. For an easy,
playful approach to take-out, simply bring in drinks in festive bottles, colorful paper goods, and delightful
Asian food boxes, and you'll be surprised how the space will transform in minutes. Take-out has never
looked so good!

intriguing shapes festive forms layered colors

ASIAN FUSION

1 WHAT IS THE OCCASION?   A birthday party for a friend or coworker.

2 ENVISION YOUR IDEAL SETTING   Fast, fun, and festive. It should be inexpensive and easy to set up. It should delight and surprise the guest of honor.

3 DEVELOP A MAKEOVER STYLE   Remembering many spontaneous "let's just get take-out" nights, I pictured mystery boxes filled with Chinese dim sum, Vietnamese spring rolls, Thai satay sticks. The mix of flavors running through my mind made me crave a taste of all, so I let eclectic cuisine decide my style: "Asian Fusion."

CHINESE CHECKERBOARD TRAY

Sometimes the most unexpected objects make great centerpieces. This old wood checkerboard is easily transformed into a tray. All it took was a quick trip to a local glass shop where they cut a piece of glass to fit the top, for only $8!

Although I used the checkerboard as a table centerpiece, it would have also worked well as a piece of art, casually leaned up against the wall on the sideboard, where it can be easily reached for a game over dessert!

4 CREATE YOUR STYLE BOARD   I wanted a vivacious, colorful look; no Zen-like neutrals or minimalist shapes for this happy bash! On a search for fun prints and colors, I headed off to the art supply store and found some great origami paper. I placed some flat on the board, and others I folded into miniature fans—so cute! I then added various Asian packages and candies and a photo of some mouth-watering spring rolls. A few colorful artificial orchids and cherry blossoms and a pair of chopsticks and my board was virtually complete!

5 PAINT YOUR COLOR PALETTE   Deepwater Blue, Snow Pea Green, Chinese Red, Orchid Yellow, and Lotus Pink sprang from an array of paper fans for my palette.

STYLING SUPPLY LIST

Dining table

White plastic folding chairs

Sideboard

Blue print cotton curtains

Paper parasols, lanterns in various sizes and colors

Parade pole with lantern top

Take-out food cartons

Blue paper place mats

Plastic plates, cups, spoons, forks, and straws

Wooden chopsticks

Chinese checkerboard tray

Miscellaneous boxes and bottles from Asian food stores

Colored teapot, vases, and figurines

Souvenir pincushion

Japanese handmade paper

Canvas, and paint

Yellow birdcage

Orchids

6 GATHER YOUR STYLING SUPPLIES   Although this makeover is based more on shopping outside the house than rummaging around inside, I still found some delightful styling supplies right on hand. I'd discovered an old Chinese checkers game at a garage sale (for $5, how could I pass it up?), and the checkerboard's classic kitschy graphics made it a perfect serving tray. A birdcage I had hidden away was exactly the right yellow and suggested chirping songbirds. My shopping trip took me first to Chinatown, where a wholesale grocery provided take-out boxes and packages of teas, soaps, and other brightly wrapped items that aligned with my color scheme. An import store had large paper parasols and lanterns and a pair of inexpensive cotton drapes just right for wall hangings. I picked up the orchids in the floral section of the grocery store on the day of the party.

fortunes **paper collage** lanterns

7 STYLE THE SPACE **LAY THE FOUNDATION** I cleared the dining room of all furniture except the sideboard and table, and pushed the sideboard back against the windows as a base for a display. White plastic folding chairs gave a more contemporary, movable-feast sort of feel.

SOFTEN THE LINES The cotton curtains from an import store went up as panels on one of the walls, immediately adding a soft wash of light blue to the room. Hanging the lanterns over the table brought the focus to the center of the room and filled in the height, seeming to almost draw the ceiling down to create a more intimate setting. Next, as a creative project that could end up as a gift for the honoree, I made a Japanese paper collage (see Style-To, below) to display on the opposite wall. I leaned the paper parade pole with lantern top in a corner for fun and to frame the tall window.

JAPANESE PAPER COLLAGE

Painter's canvas, any size (from an art store)

Japanese wrapping paper in various prints and colors (at least three different papers per canvas)

Small jar of acrylic paint in a coordinating or neutral color

Decoupage glue

Scissors

❖ Paint the edge of the canvas to finish it off. Don't worry about getting the paint on the front as you'll cover it with the paper.

❖ For each piece of artwork, start by choosing three different colored papers. Two will be for your background, and the third will be for your object.

❖ Measure the entire canvas, cut one paper to that size, and glue it down leaving the painted edges showing.

❖ Cut another paper to cover approximately the bottom third of the canvas and glue it on top of the first one.

❖ With a freehand or stencil, draw or trace an object (teapot, chopsticks, bowl, flower) out of the third color of paper. Then cut and glue the object on the canvas, allowing it to slightly overlap the bottom piece of paper. This gives the illusion that your object is sitting on a tabletop.

FABRIC WALL HANGING

Tape lightweight cotton curtains to the wall using blue tape painters which generally won't remove paint. Hide the tape on the underside. If your material is heavier, you might consider using pushpins.

PERSONALIZE WITH DETAILS Now for the decorative tabletop elements and all those shopping bags filled with goodies. With the yellow birdcage as a focal point, I styled the sideboard with a cheerful jumble of pretty boxes and bottles, stacking them in eccentric ways until they looked just right. I made an unexpected centerpiece for the table by turning my checkerboard into a tray and slipping it under a fun porcelain figurine. A small pincushion became the menu holder, and sprays of graceful orchids added an elegant touch.

8 STYLE THE FOOD AND TABLE   I set each place setting with a blue paper place mat and two white plastic plates in different sizes, topped with a green napkin, a take-out box, and chopsticks, building each setting up for height. A green plastic cup and spoon and a soda bottle with a bright pink plastic straw completed each place setting. The spring rolls were homemade but served in the take-out boxes to add a postmodern twist. A pyramid of fortune cookies on a plate at the end of the table tantalized guests, who knew their secret destinies were only a meal away. And for the grand finale, green tea ice cream scooped into mint-green plastic cups and decorated with tiny orchids.

VIETNAMESE-STYLE SPRING ROLLS WITH DIPPING SAUCE

For the rolls

1 package spring roll wrappers (rice paper)

3/4 cup bean sprouts

2 ounces cooked vermicelli noodles

1/3 cup fresh basil

1/3 cup fresh mint

1/3 cup fresh cilantro

24 cooked, shelled shrimp

1 cup fresh spinach

Soak the rice-paper wrappers in a shallow dish of cold water until soft (approximately 2 minutes).

To assemble, beginning 1 inch from one end, lay a small amount of bean sprouts, cooked noodles, and fresh herbs on the rice paper. Roll the extra inch of rice paper over the filling and place a line of three shrimp on top. Place spinach over shrimp and roll up firmly. Continue until you have made eight rolls. Serve with Ponzu Ginger dipping sauce.

SERVES FOUR

PONZU GINGER DIPPING SAUCE

2 tablespoons ponzu sauce
$1/2$ teaspoon soy sauce
$1/2$ teaspoon lime juice
$1/8$ teaspoon freshly grated ginger
1 clove garlic, pressed
1 small red chili, sliced
pinch of sugar

Combine all ingredients and serve with spring rolls.

CHAPTER 4

*Stepping out the back door
and onto the patio doesn't have to
be a dreaded experience. The following
patio makeovers show you how to turn
your plain concrete slab into almost
anything! With a little imaginative
styling, you can have a soft, intimate
setting with a French flair, a colorful
Fourth of July–inspired set-up for
summer barbeques, and a lush tropical
getaway—perfect for celebrating
a special occasion.*

O

FRENCH LAUNDRY

STAR-SPANGLED SUMMER

TROPICAL PARADISE

My casual entertaining makeover, "French Laundry," illustrates how easily you can transcend patio tedium by styling an outdoor room using indoor furniture (like a daybed) and fabrics (like white cotton and lace)—the **best of both** worlds. This fresh and invitingly intimate spot is wonderful for afternoon reading and visiting with friends. ✺ Summer is prime patio time, so mark the season and shake up the place with a "Star-Spangled Summer" makeover. With an amusing array of cast-off household items, some bright paint, **lots of imagination,** and a moderate supply of elbow grease, you can style a smile for everyone who stops to take a turn on the swing. It's a perfect setup to carry the family through the summer. ✺ What about creating a "Tropical Paradise" getaway out of that concrete jungle? Impossible? Not at all! This makeover is a perfect setup for a **special occasion** your guests won't soon forget (and you can leave the makeover in place and enjoy fresh breakfasts beneath the palm tree). The all-out use of colors and textures—from a container-based garden to fencing and floor coverings—creates an **island oasis** right outside your door.

FRENCH LAUNDRY

A simple laundry line inspires a backdrop of beauty for a special lunch.

THE FRENCH HAVE A KNACK FOR FINDING THE MOST PICTURESQUE OF PLACES IN WHICH TO PERFORM the most mundane of chores. For this makeover, imagine a country home outside Paris, formerly the stable for a grand chateau. In the kitchen there is a long farm table and cheese boards on the sideboard. Just outside, in the sunshine, you envision chairs and a table surrounded by flowers and trees. C'est magnifique, non? But now add a few more domestic details, some breezes and light, a laundry line hung with sweet-smelling linens and fresh, clean clothes. Voilà. In this setting, children devour bread and chocolate and play tag among the warm sheets that flap in the summer air. Mais oui!

country elegance picturesque light breezes

FABRIC SCREEN

Wood screen

Batting or thin foam (enough to cover the panels of the screen)

Fabric of your choice (enough to cover the panels of the screen)

Hot glue gun

Staple gun

Trim (enough to edge all the fabric panels on the screen)

※ Measure the panels of the screen inside the frames.

※ Cut the batting or foam to fit each panel of the screen, and glue on.

※ Cut the material to fit the size of each panel, leaving an extra inch on all sides to fold over frame.

※ Fold over the extra inch of fabric and iron to crease. This will create a clean edge when you staple it to the screen.

※ Lay the screen down and place the fabric over the batting or foam. Staple the fabric to the inside edge of the wood screen. Make sure that the fabric is straight and staples are parallel and as close to the edge of the fabric as possible.

※ If needed, finish by gluing a trim, rope, or rolled piece of the coordinating fabric around the edges to cover the staples.

1 WHAT IS THE OCCASION?   A quiet tête-à-tête between friends, then a few hours alone with a book.

2 ENVISION YOUR IDEAL SETTING   This everyday space should serve both as a place to entertain à deux and a hideaway for solo reveries. This patio would also be great as a sleeping porch—as comfortable and intimate as a bedroom—with pillows, cushions, linens, and lace in place of typical patio furniture.

3 DEVELOP A MAKEOVER STYLE   A white ceramic washbasin from a flea market and a simple laundry line inspired a beautiful backdrop for this special lunch. Thinking of all things airy and fresh, I landed on the image of "French Laundry."

4 CREATE YOUR STYLE BOARD   I started by pinning up a fabric sample of burgundy-and-white toile that was extremely French. Some postcard-sized reproductions of French Impressionist paintings of laundresses at work and women putting up their hair seemed to capture the mood, so tout suite, up they went. My Style File yielded a tear sheet from a gardening magazine of several different delicate, lacy-leafed plants and a newspaper recipe for salade niçoise. Finally, for a more literal representation of my style, I added a little length of white clothesline.

5 PAINT YOUR COLOR PALETTE   Linen au Naturel, Pinot Rouge Burgundy, Ivoire White, and Parisian Pink formed a color scheme that reminded me of a French Impressionist painting.

6 GATHER YOUR STYLING SUPPLIES   A daybed is the foundation of this makeover, and there are many ways to get one. The piece pictured here is a flea-market find of white wrought

STYLING SUPPLY LIST

Rustic white wrought iron daybed

White porcelain baby basin

Wrought iron trellises

Wooden screen

Folding table or any odd table

White and burgundy sheets

Gauze fabric

White vintage garments and string

Linen potato sacks

Linen tablecloth

Potato vine plants, maidenhair ferns, and pink flowers

Metal and wicker baskets and accessories

Old-fashioned bar of soap

Mini clothesline and notecards

Vintage laundry soap container

Notecards

iron, but you may have an old wooden bed frame that you can paint white and distress, or you could find an inexpensive metal frame and simply flop a mattress onto it. Next, look around for a table—any weathered odd table will come in handy. Gather up everything you can find that's made of wrought iron—a plant stand, gate, or wine rack—and collect old sheets, a few baskets, and some distinctively French fabric, tea towels, or tablecloths. If you don't have any toile on hand, buy some at a fabric store. Other small purchases, like some inexpensive wooden clothespins or a couple of distinctive plants, contribute charm to the atmosphere.

au natural impressionist tout suite

7 STYLE THE SPACE **LAY THE FOUNDATION** I placed the iron daybed between the house and the corner post, then stood two wrought iron trellises to the side of the bed as well as directly opposite on the other side of the patio to create a feeling of enclosure. These wrought iron pieces were placed at a 90-degree angle and then attached with plastic ties, which allowed them to stand on the patio without any other anchor. Across from the daybed I added a large urn and laundry basket. A vintage baby basin became a planter; a table within arm's reach of the daybed provided for a lounger's every need.

SOFTEN THE LINE. Now for the fun! This patio, with its hard-edged rectangular lines, really needed some help to soften its profile and create a more intimate setting, so I added fabric and plants at every opportunity. A floral toile screen (see Style-To, p. 114) provided the perfect colorful backdrop to the daybed. I then covered the bed with a burgundy-striped sheet and accented it with my new potato-sack pillows (see Style-To, right). I found a small natural cotton tablecloth with a burgundy stripe to cover the table. The clothesline, with its vintage "laundry," created another screen as well as some shade. White gauze panels of fabric, just off a bolt and thrown loosely over the French doors to sway in the breeze, added movement and a timeless, romantic look. I created a faux arbor above the daybed by positioning two large potato vine plants on either side, and draping them with the assistance of a wire strung between the house and the post. For an unusual but pretty accent, I folded a pile of fresh clean sheets into the wicker laundry basket.

OLD FRENCH POTATO SACK PILLOWS

Old French potato sacks, or natural-linen-colored pillowcases
Standard bed pillows
Ribbon or twine

☼ Simply place your pillow inside the potato sack (I like to leave an old pillowcase on the pillow), and tie off the end with ribbon or twine. Potato Sack Pillows can be used anywhere. They are an excellent styling tool, as they immediately soften the space.

BASKETS OF LAUNDRY

Stacked baskets piled with old white sheets help to lend reality to this makeover. Sheets are not an item you would normally think to bring out to the patio, but it's these unexpected touches that add style and character.

CLOTHESLINE MENU HOLDER

Wood glue

*Four 1-by-1 1/2-inch pieces
  of wood*

Two 1-by-4-inch pieces of wood

*Two 1-foot-long 3/4-inch
  wooden dowels with a small
  hole through one end*

Small nails

Hammer

1 foot of string

Note card

Old doll's clothes

Mini wooden clothespins

❋ Glue two of the 1-by-
1 1/2-inch wood pieces across
from each other to the
center of a 1-by-4-inch piece
to form a flat cross base.

❋ Center the first pole and
nail it to the base.

❋ Repeat to make the
second base and pole.

❋ Run the string through
the holes at the top of the
poles and tie off.

❋ Write out your menu on
the note card.

❋ Hang the menu and the
doll's clothes on the line
with the mini clothespins.

PERSONALIZE WITH DETAILS Small details set the stage for a special lunch between friends, so I strung up a miniature laundry line and hung a menu card with a clothespin (see Style-To, left). As whimsical props, I put out bars of soap and a laundry soap container. The Parisian pink in the flowers and lunch dishes underscored the feminine feel.

8 STYLE THE FOOD AND TABLE   Collecting a variety of old china pieces from flea markets and thrift stores is always a great start for styling the table—these items can add instant character to any occasion. I served the salad as well as the dessert on pink floral flea-market finds and finished by stacking pieces of chocolate as high as they could go without toppling on a coordinating pedestal dish. Bring out several lovely liqueur glasses for the pastis.

SALADE NIÇOISE

1 cup green beans

1 head butter lettuce

4 hardboiled eggs, chopped (whites only)

2 tomatoes, seeded and chopped

1/2 red onion, thinly sliced

1 cup kalamata olives

1 pound fresh tuna steaks (can also substitute canned tuna)

1/4 cup Italian parsley, chopped

Trim and blanch the beans in boiling water for 4 minutes, then cut into 2-inch pieces.

Wash and dry the lettuce and tear bite-size pieces into a large bowl. (Tearing the lettuce, a common French technique, prevents damage to the leaves.) Add the blanched beans, egg whites, tomatoes, onions, and olives. Toss and place on individual salad plates or bowls.

Sear the tuna on high heat in a nonstick pan for approximately 3 minutes. (The tuna is seared when the outside is slightly browned and the inside is still deep pink.) Slice and add to individual salads. Drizzle with dressing and sprinkle with parsley.

SERVES FOUR

French Vinaigrette Dressing

2 tablespoons Dijon mustard

1/2 cup red wine vinegar

1 cup vegetable oil

2 teaspoons Herbes de Provence

1 teaspoon salt

Mix the Dijon mustard and red wine vinegar together first. (This will allow for a more thorough blending of ingredients.) Add the oil, Herbes de Provence, salt, and whisk until combined.

PAIN AU CHOCOLAT

1 French baguette

1 pound bar of fine quality milk chocolate

Cut the baguette into four pieces and slice each in half down the middle.

Make sure the chocolate is at room temperature. Using a sharp knife, carefully shave chocolate onto each piece of bread (the right amount is purely up to your taste buds).

Serve with a chilled glass of pastis (an anise-scented liqueur) for a grown-up accompaniment to this luscious afternoon treat. For the kids, serve with hot chocolate. It's perfect for dipping!

SERVES FOUR

MENU
GRILLED CHICKEN SANDWICHES WITH PESTO MAYONNAISE
CORN ON THE COB WITH CHILI-LIME BUTTER
STRAWBERRIES AND CREAM WITH WAFER COOKIES
ASSORTED BOTTLED SODAS AND FRUIT DRINKS

STAR-SPANGLED SUMMER

*Reuse, recycle, renew your stashed-away items. With your own odds and ends,
you can style a fun patio for the whole family to enjoy.*

HAVE YOU EVER NOTICED HOW A YARD SALE PROVIDES SUCH ENTER-
TAINMENT FOR KIDS, playing with long-forgotten toys, sitting in quirky old chairs,
or making a playhouse out of whatever they find at hand? Wouldn't it be great if we could keep
that gift of effortless creativity into adulthood?

Here's a refresher for your spirit. This star-spangled patio makeover brings the breeze of youth and
improvisation to a carefree setting that will keep you smiling throughout the season. You'll be inspired to light
up the grill every night when you see the reminder of bright fireworks of the Fourth of July.

carefree **fireworks** star-spangled

EIGHT STEPS TO
STAR-SPANGLED SUMMER

WHEELBARROW WATER FOUNTAIN

This homemade fountain doubles as a drink cooler for parties.

Metal wheelbarrow

6 bricks (amount will vary depending on depth of the wheelbarrow)

Toy tractor

Small water pump (can be purchased at a garden store or nursery)

3–4 feet of plastic tubing

Outdoor extension cord

☀ Place the pump with the tubing attached in the center of the wheelbarrow.

☀ Mound the bricks over the pump and place the toy tractor on top.

☀ Pull the base end of the tubing up through the top of the pile of bricks and through your tractor so that the water will spout out the top.

☀ Fill the wheelbarrow with water, plug the pump into an electrical outlet, and turn on.

☀ To use as a cooler, fill the wheelbarrow with ice and load up with drinks. When the ice melts turn on the pump and let the kids enjoy the fountain.

1 WHAT IS THE OCCASION?   Summer's here—it's time for family fun and an endless barbecue!

2 ENVISION YOUR IDEAL SETTING   A bright spot for casual summer entertaining. The furniture and accessories should be tough enough to withstand a summer's worth of exuberant child's play, with no worries about mishaps or spills by kids or crazy grown-ups.

3 DEVELOP A MAKEOVER STYLE   There's no better way to achieve an inexpensive fresh look than by bringing new life to old objects, something I do all the time with flea-market finds. So I decided to make "star-spangled recycling" the style for this makeover. Hey, there's gotta be a way to get some use out of all of that junk . . . er, stuff . . . um, collectibles?

4 CREATE YOUR STYLE BOARD   Since this was a seasonal makeover, I scoured my Style File for summer images and picked out a picture of a park bandstand draped in red, white, and blue bunting as well as photos from a summer road trip: white picket fences with red geraniums, roadside stands offering fresh-picked corn, and kids at a lemonade stand. For a party menu, I made a list of family barbecue favorites (grilled chicken, corn on the cob) and tacked it up. Ever the flavor maven, I added some simple recipes (chili-lime butter, pesto mayonnaise) that would give these familiar dishes a different twist.

STYLING SUPPLY LIST

Red, white, blue, and yellow paint	Stars-and-stripes tablecloth
Wooden and metal table and chairs	Metal tins, canisters, and buckets
Children's furniture	Vintage metal kitchen utensils
Baker's rack	Plastic serving baskets
Bench swing	Child's garden boots
Ladder	Assorted vintage toys, dolls, and games
White picket fence	Geraniums
Wagon	
Wheelbarrow	
Wooden ironing board	
Old wood shutters	
Wooden toolbox	
Colorful linens	

5 PAINT YOUR COLOR PALETTE   To Apple Red, Picket-Fence White, and True Blue, I added a fourth color, Sunshine Yellow, because I liked the bright accent. Stepping back to look at my Style Board, I saw the all-American Fourth of July colors that roped me in. If I used this patriotic palette, the patio would not only be fresh for the summer, but also ready for the holiday.

6 GATHER YOUR STYLING SUPPLIES   I began my styling process by piling a big basket with everything I could find in red, white, blue, or yellow. This included vintage-inspired flowered linens, red-checked dish towels, a stars-and-stripes tablecloth, a child's red wagon, red plastic cups and serving baskets, some painted metal bowls, and a roll of yellow-checked Con-Tact paper. For basic furniture, I liked the white bench swing that was already on the patio, plus a friendly old table with chipped paint and some farmhouse chairs. I gathered some toys that would make the kids feel at home. Next, I looked around for odds and ends to recycle in the attic, basement, and

white picket fences **recycled treasures** breeze of youth

garage (you can also hunt yard sales and flea markets), keeping my eyes open for things like mis-matched wooden and metal furniture, old tins, bins, and buckets, and cast-off toys and playthings. Among my finds were several that I decided to repaint or repurpose: a stepladder (painted red, it became a plant shelf), a wooden ironing board (painted blue and yellow), a buffet table, a small section of picket fencing (red, white, and blue paint created an eye-catching entrance), an old red wheelbarrow that turned into a drinks cooler and water fountain. Perhaps you have or come across similar treasures—a gate, old farm implements, a mailbox, maybe a washtub or vintage milk can. By painting these disparate items in the colors you've selected for your palette, you can create a unified style.

7 STYLE THE SPACE   **LAY THE FOUNDATION** Because this makeover was so color-driven, I wasted no time in laying down newspaper and pulling out my brushes and paint. I didn't plan ahead, but just started by painting one chair blue and another yellow. Hmm, my baker's rack would look nice in yellow, too. And what about the stepladder and ironing board? I opted for red on the ladder simply because I liked the idea of a red ladder, and chose blue and yellow for the ironing board. Why not? Terra-cotta pots: bright yellow. Picket fence: red, white, and blue. There was no method to the painting madness—just lots of color and a new look for each piece.

GARDEN BOOT PLANTERS

Pair of colorful child's garden boots

Two plants of your choice, in 3- or 4-inch plastic pots

☼ Punch a few holes in the bottom of each boot for drainage. If not, make sure you remove the plant when watering so the roots don't get waterlogged.

☼ Keep the plants in the plastic pots and place one in each boot. If your plants and pots are smaller than the boot's width and sink to the bottom, prop them up with a base of gravel or small rocks.

After the recycled pieces had dried, I marked a colorful gated entrance with the freshly painted picket fence. I placed the children's and adult's tables just a stone's throw away from one another, as kids love their own separate area—as do we adults! The freshly painted stepladder with attached shelf went next to add height and to enclose the corner of the patio, while the baker's rack zipped into the back, where it would add personality but stay out of the kids' way as they zoomed in and out. The ironing board was placed to the side, where it would make a great buffet table, and I set up the red wheelbarrow in the center so its contents could easily be reached. It was going to be doubly recycled—I was making it into a water fountain that would double as a drink cooler (see Style-To, p. 126).

SOFTEN THE LINES   To make a colorful backdrop for the patio and separate the interior and exterior of the house, I draped several tablecloths of vintage 1940s flower-print cotton over the windows. Tablecloths also graced the kids' and adults' tables as well as the ironing-board buffet table. A small rag rug near the picket fence warmed up the concrete underfoot, and a large potted plant just inside the fence helped define the enclosure. I brought more life to the setting in this step by bringing in other brightly potted plants. Nothing softens the look of a hard metal baker's rack like velvety geraniums! I then turned some children's garden boots into planters (see Style-To, p. 131) and placed them along with a weathered birdhouse on the stepladder and shelf.

PERSONALIZE WITH DETAILS   After the overall layout was established (in a purposefully casual and deceptively random fashion!), it was time to bring in the small items. I gathered canisters, toys, and baskets and bowls and spread them around in an unstructured way. My only plan was that the bright colors should ultimately bring an absolutely delightful cheeriness to the space. The toys went into the wagon next to the entrance. Everything looked great except for the bench swing, which seemed a little stark until I sat Raggedy Ann and Andy there to smile at one and all.

8 STYLE THE FOOD AND TABLE   Still having fun with my plan to recycle as many objects as I could, I lined a wooden toolbox with yellow-checked Con-Tact paper to use as a serving tray. The fresh berries, after being washed, went back into their cartons and then into the toolbox—how vibrant the red berries looked against the yellow checks! Red and yellow plastic baskets provided a colorful way to serve the chicken sandwiches, and red plastic utensils and cups fit right into the palette, style, and season. I served the strawberries in plastic wineglasses topped with fresh whipped cream and a wafer cookie to add a touch of simple elegance.

IRONING BOARD BUFFET TABLE

This recycled ironing board —given a facelift with a coat of fresh blue paint—makes a great buffet table, and surely shows that a little creativity goes a long way.

GRILLED CHICKEN SANDWICH WITH PESTO MAYONNAISE

4 small skinless, boneless chicken breasts

1/4 cup olive oil

1 tablespoon vinegar

1/2 teaspoon salt

Freshly ground pepper to taste

8 slices sourdough bread

4 leaves green leaf lettuce

2 tomatoes, sliced

Pesto Mayonnaise

3 tablespoons mayonnaise

1 tablespoon store-bought pesto

Mix together mayonnaise and pesto. Set aside.

Combine olive oil, vinegar, salt, and pepper and brush over chicken breasts. Grill until thoroughly cooked.

Toast bread briefly on the grill and spread each piece with pesto mayonnaise. Add the grilled chicken breast, and top with sliced tomato and lettuce. Sprinkle with salt and pepper. Serve warm.

SERVES FOUR

CORN ON THE COB WITH CHILI-LIME BUTTER

2 small mild red chilies, finely chopped

2 tablespoons butter, softened

1 teaspoon cumin

4 ears fresh sweet corn, husked

1 lime, quartered

Salt and freshly ground pepper to taste

Mash two-thirds of the chilies with the butter and cumin in a bowl to form a paste.

Cook the corn in boiling water for 2 to 4 minutes, then grill, turning occasionally until slightly charred on all sides.

Place corn on serving dish and rub each ear with chili butter. Season with salt, pepper, the remaining chopped chilies, and a squeeze of lime.

SERVES FOUR

STRAWBERRIES AND CREAM
WITH WAFER COOKIES

For an easy, delicious strawberry desert, simply slice fresh strawberries, place in plastic wine glass and top with fresh whipped cream and a wafer cookie.

If the strawberries need some extra sweetening, sprinkle with a bit of white sugar.

TROPICAL PARADISE

Bring back memories of an island vacation with this lush patio makeover for an anniversary celebration.

WHAT IS IT ABOUT A TROPICAL ISLAND GETAWAY THAT IS SO ALLURING? The warm turquoise sea—your toes in the hot sand—and dozing off in the afternoon sun. When you get home from that vacation you long for those wonderful moments. You look out your back door and the patio looks nothing like that wonderful rain forest resort. What if you could just bring a bit of that vacation paradise to your own home? It's easier than you think to transform your concrete jungle into a tropical oasis. With a few fragrant flowers, lush greenery, some lively island colors, and a dash of summer sun you can experience paradise in your own backyard.

hammock sarongs and pareos barefoot relaxing

TROPICAL PARADISE

1 WHAT IS THE OCCASION?   An anniversary party.

2 ENVISION YOUR IDEAL SETTING   A patio set-up allowing guests to savor the longer daylight hours and soft evening breezes of late spring and early summer. Not only will this makeover create a memorable setting for the party, but it can also live on as the basis of a year-round style for this space. A sheltered patio area is perfect for creating an indoor-outdoor feeling, and this one should be sophisticated, more like a resort than a backyard.

3 DEVELOP A MAKEOVER STYLE   A lush garden with everything from palm trees and luxuriant, big-leaved plants to dazzling arrays of tropical fruits. This one was easy—"Tropical Paradise!"

TROPICAL PLANT PALETTE

Look for color, texture, and unusual shapes when choosing your plant material. Some examples from this makeover that provided interest are:

- ☀ Asparagus Ferns
- ☀ Philodendron
- ☀ Canna
- ☀ Palms
- ☀ Birds
- ☀ Cycads
- ☀ Bromeliads
- ☀ Protea

4 CREATE YOUR STYLE BOARD   This one started with a small sample of bamboo fencing—because what island resort doesn't incorporate bamboo into its design? With vibrant colors, a key element of my makeover, I tacked up a fuchsia napkin near the bottom and a paper napkin in mango and orange in the top corner. The napkins provided a colorful backdrop for the other items I would be scattering on the board. A small tiki torch, some tear sheets of tropical entertaining set-ups, and a few tropical leaves and flowers and I was beginning to clearly see my image of paradise. As a final touch, I attached a couple of drink umbrellas that would accompany my island beverages.

STYLING SUPPLY LIST

Palapa or large patio umbrella with thatching

Bamboo fencing

Two roll-up bamboo window shades

Small teak table

Serving cart

Wooden trough and stool

Lengths of bamboo

Rattan chairs

Sisal or sea-grass rug

Galvanized tub and small water pump

Green-and-pink throw pillows

Mango and pink glassware

Pink tropical print napkins

Bamboo tray

Bamboo water pitcher

Yellow, pink, green, and orange candles

Palms, birds-of-paradise, canna, asparagus fern, bromeliads, proteas

Glazed pots in earth tones

Mini tiki torches

Assorted tropical fruits

5 PAINT YOUR COLOR PALETTE   Hot Hibiscus Pink, Mango, Banana Yellow, and Palm-Leaf Green. I decided to spotlight the two brightest colors, the hot pink and mango, against the lush green, and to add elements of rattan, sisal, bamboo, jute, and teak for texture (an important aspect of this makeover).

6 GATHER YOUR STYLING SUPPLIES   The *palapa* (an open-sided, thatched-roof structure), bamboo fencing, and sisal or sea grass rug form the main backdrop for this tropical patio, so they go at the top of your styling supply list. If you can't find a *palapa,* use a patio umbrella by itself or attach some thatching, which you can find premade or make yourself with palm fronds or grass hula skirts tied on the top. Bamboo fencing is an inexpensive and very effective screening material available at home and garden stores; together with the sea-grass or sisal rug underfoot, it helps to bring back memories of warm, palm-shaded islands. You get a lot of luxury for your investment

with rattan, teak, and bamboo furniture, which (like the large potted tropical plants) can be used indoors or out when you decide to change things around. Check import and home improvement stores for bamboo shades, mini tiki torches, and the supplies needed to make a tropical water fountain. Fruit is always a great styling supply, and mangoes, guavas, passion fruit, pineapples, lemons, limes, coconuts with their grassy shells, and of course bananas all add a Caribbean flavor to this makeover. (Plus you can feast on them after the party.) Gather up large wood serving bowls, trays, or platters and pile it on with abundance!

BAMBOO WATER FOUNTAIN

Galvanized tub

Small water pump

60 inches of plastic tubing to fit your water pump

Two 30-inch pieces of bamboo, approx. $1/2$ inch in diameter

Eight 18-inch pieces of bamboo, approx. $1/2$ inch in diameter

Small pot filled with sand

Twine

Enough medium-sized gravel to cover bottom of tub

1 outdoor-rated extension cord

2 pieces short bamboo fencing, just tall enough to hide the tub's sides and equal in length to the tub's circumference

※ Place the tub where you'd like your water feature to be.

※ To create the bamboo spout, place three 18-inch pieces of bamboo around the tubing at one end, making sure that the end of the tubing is flush with the end of the bamboo. Tie together by wrapping in three or four places with twine. Bend the exposed tubing and attach to it the two 30-inch pieces of bamboo, creating an angle. Secure with twine. Finally, splint the last two 18-inch pieces of bamboo between the first two groupings and tie with twine to hold them in place. This creates the triangle shape you'll see in the photo.

※ Camouflage the outside (and, if you like, the inside) of the tub with bamboo fencing, wiring the ends together to secure it.

※ Anchor the base of the bamboo spout in a pot filled with sand, behind the tub.

※ Place the pump in the tub and hook the end of the tubing to the pump.

※ Run the cord of the pump over the edge of the tub and plug it in to an outdoor-rated extension cord.

※ Cover the bottom of the tub with small river rocks and fill it with water.

※ Plug in and enjoy.

STYLING WITH FRUIT

Fruits make an excellent styling supply—especially for a tropical makeover. They provide bright colors, varying textures, and tantalizing aromas. Experiment with different arrangements, working with your color palette. If one doesn't work, you can always snack on it while you figure out a fruit that does!

7 STYLE THE SPACE **LAY THE FOUNDATION** I placed the *palapa* first, as it was the largest item and anchored the makeover, leaving room for plants and the bamboo fencing behind. Grouping a low teak table with two rattan chairs gave a start to an intimate seating area, to which I added another chair and a teak serving cart that could double as a bar. To enhance the rain-forest effect with its sensual bubbling sound, I made a bamboo fountain (see Style-To, p. 143) for the water element that's essential to any tropical scene. And to establish one of the boundaries—I wanted the space enclosed on three sides—I positioned a wooden trough at one edge of the patio, ready to be filled with a colorful display of tropical fruit.

SOFTEN THE LINES The large jute rug went down first—not under the *palapa,* mind you, as it would be pinned there forever, but instead butted up against the base of the stand. A smaller jute rug (available at import and home stores) on the other side of the stand filled in the remaining space. I then sectioned off the back to enclose the tropical area by unrolling the bamboo fencing and securing it between two posts. To soften the windows and door and further define my little paradise, I hung two inexpensive bamboo shades. Arranging a dozen tropical plants behind the *palapa* and around the water feature created an instant garden; I replanted some into large earth-tone glazed pots and left the others in their plastic pots, camouflaged with a bit of low premade bamboo fence; then I placed the taller plants to the rear and the smaller ones in front, so the greenery flowed down to the edge of the rug. Pillows and seat cushions in rich, colorful fabrics contrasted beautifully with the wood and bamboo.

PERSONALIZE WITH DETAILS Tropical gardens are always chockablock with large leafy plants that make big statements. Since mine was no exception, I wanted to keep small items to a minimum. Too many knickknacks would make the area seem kitschy rather than elegant and detract attention from the organic surfaces of the bamboo, palm, jute, and wood. This step was as simple as placing candles in tropical colors on the table, on the cart, and on a small stool, then adding a few mini tiki torches. The romantic flickering of flames added that wonderful sunset glow.

8 STYLE THE FOOD AND TABLE I now introduced some brightly colored glassware and serving platters to add a tropical splash to the table. These can be glass or plastic. Dare to indulge in shades you may normally shy away from. Offer the iced tea in two different colors of glasses garnished with fresh fruit, then choose another fruit or two to adorn the fish plates. Papaya and watermelon served for dessert continue the yellow-pink color scheme, but if your colors are orange and green, for example, you may want to finish the meal with oranges and kiwi instead!

ISLAND BAKED RED SNAPPER

1/2 cup of Ketjap Manis sauce (Indonesian soy sauce, available in ethnic grocery stores, or substitute regular soy sauce)

1/2 cup white balsamic vinegar

1 finely chopped red chili, seeded

1 clove garlic, pressed

1 teaspoon finely grated fresh ginger

3 limes

2 small whole red snapper, cleaned, scaled, and gutted (you may also substitute filets of a mild white fish such as ono)

Preheat oven to 425°.

For the marinade, whisk together the Ketjap Manis or soy sauce, vinegar, chili, garlic, ginger, and the juice of two limes.

Set snapper in a baking dish lined with aluminum foil. Thinly slice the third lime and place inside the fish. Pour marinade over fish, cover, and refrigerate for half an hour or more. Remove from refrigerator and bake for 25 to 30 minutes. Garnish with fresh herbs and lime.

SERVES FOUR

MANGO AND ARUGULA SALAD WITH CHILI AND LIME

8 ounces fresh baby arugula (substitute watercress, if desired)

2 ripe but firm mangoes, peeled and sliced

Dressing

4 tablespoons olive oil

3 tablespoons white wine vinegar

3 tablespoons lime juice

1 tablespoon sugar

1 small red chili, chopped

2 teaspoons freshly chopped mint

2–3 dashes hot sauce (optional)

1 teaspoon salt

1 teaspoon freshly ground pepper

Whisk together the dressing ingredients and let sit in refrigerator for several hours to allow flavors to combine.

Place the arugula in a large bowl, pour over half the dressing, and gently toss. Make individual servings on salad plates or bowls by placing a handful of arugula and arranging the mango slices on top. Drizzle each salad with some of the remaining dressing and garnish with fresh mint leaves and red chili slices.

SERVES FOUR

THE LA

W N

CHAPTER 5

*A big, grassy backyard is great
for a game of croquet, but it can be
overwhelming when you're planning an
outdoor gathering. If you think of your
lawn as a blank green canvas, however,
you can immediately see that your
styling options are endless.*

*These makeovers make use of
one easy-to-build structure as the
foundation for three very different
looks. Based on outdoor buildings that
appear in different places throughout the
world, from English estate gazebos to
the warm-weather pavilions of Indian
rajahs, this backyard addition provides
a versatile entertaining space and
brings style to your property.*

ENGLISH TEA GARDEN

BEFORE

AFTER

EXOTIC OASIS

CHAMPAGNE WEDDING

"English Tea Garden," my casual makeover, creates a sweet trellised rose garden within the greater expanse of lawn. Containers filled with flowering plants can be changed with the season so you never tire of your **backyard retreat.** Even better, this gorgeous setting can be ready at a moment's notice to receive your guests for afternoon tea. ❋ It's a long way from the English countryside to the Moroccan desert, but it only takes a day to make the transition in your own backyard. The **vibrant styling** of the "Exotic Oasis" makeover is designed for those late summer afternoons that stretch long into evening. The same trellis forms the foundation here, but when it's draped with glorious fabric in rich, bright colors, the rose garden becomes a **caravan tent** beneath the sheltering sky. ❋ Do the words simple backyard wedding translate in your mind to "expensive, backbreaking feat requiring big budget, caterer, wedding consultant, and rented tent"? Destress yourself with the special-occasion makeover "Champagne Wedding." Now your structure becomes a **wedding altar,** and all you have to rent are the chairs! Ah, breathe...

ENGLISH TEA GARDEN

*Create this lovely garden-within-a-garden, and you'll be ready to invite friends over for tea
at the drop of a ribbon-trimmed hat.*

ENGLISH TEATIME GETS A BREATH OF FRESH AIR WHEN IT'S SERVED IN AN AMERICAN BACKYARD—vivid proof that even the daintiest of rituals can be transported outdoors. Brew a strong cup of fragrant tea, pour it into your prettiest flowered porcelain teacup, and indulge in a little reverie about a secret rose garden in a corner of English countryside. You butter a crumpet as a dear friend settles in for a good gossip. She's brought you some cuttings from that rosebush with peach-colored blossoms you've been pining for. You've laid out an especially tasty spread. The sun slants through the gazebo lattice, and songbirds swoop down to splash in the birdbath as you ask her whether she'd like one lump of sugar, or two.

gazebo lattice **fragrant ritual** songbird splash

Roses come in many different varieties. Why not indulge your most primal sense and fill your garden with wonderfully scented roses? Try some of the following, as they are favorites of rosarians for fragrance:

❀ Madame Isaac Pereire (raspberry purple)

❀ Henri Martin (crimson red)

❀ Reine des Violettes (deep violet purple)

❀ Rose de Rescht (bright fuchsia)

❀ Darlow's Enigma (white)

❀ Crepuscule (gold)

❀ Double Delight (red/white blend)

❀ Belle Isis (medium pink)

❀ Alpine Sunset (apricot)

❀ Arthur Bell (chrome yellow)

❀ Alba Semiplena (white)

❀ Ferdinand Pichard (pink/crimson)

1 WHAT IS THE OCCASION?   This is an an everyday setup to have morning coffee or afternoon tea.

2 ENVISION YOUR IDEAL SETTING   A verdant garden spot on the lawn is set aside as a quiet and comfortable retreat, somewhere to sit and chat with friends or read. It should be private but open to the afternoon light, and surrounded by lots of fragrant flowers.

3 DEVELOP A MAKEOVER STYLE   As I thought about how to set off one area of a large lawn and make it private and enclosed, the pictures in my Style File of white gazebos on English country estates suggested the structural element. Then a newly opened peach-colored rose from my neighbor's bush called out the essential idea: a trellised "English Tea Garden."

4 CREATE YOUR STYLE BOARD   I pinned a petal from a rose onto my Style Board. I loved the color, softness, and romance that it conveyed. I then surrounded it with the photos I'd pulled from my Style File. Leafing through a catalog of roses, I cut out several photos of striking varieties and attached them as well. Just Joey, a large full-head apricot rose; Comte de Chambord with its silvery pink fragrant blooms; Yves Piaget's large ruffled mauve blooms; and Abraham Darby with its soft pink-lavender color, were my four top choices. A white linen napkin added the accent of a formal tea, and some tiny white satin rosettes chimed in with sleek, smooth texture. I took a hint from the classic English tea and crumpets and tacked up a shot of a shortcake piled high with fresh billowing whipped cream.

STYLING SUPPLY LIST

Materials to build the structure (see Style-To)

Premade white picket fencing

Lattice

Large white fountain

Birdbath

Wrought iron café table and chairs

White linens and floral seat cushions

Potted rose trees and other plants

Terra-cotta pots

Artificial ivy and roses

White paint

Delicate cups and saucers

Silver tea service and flatware

Loose tea

sense of history **peach rose petals** sunlight

5 PAINT YOUR COLOR PALETTE   Pale Peach, Garden Green, and Alabaster White—my Style Board made the choice of colors plain as a sunny summer's day.

6 GATHER YOUR STYLING SUPPLIES   Many of us have inherited a few genteel teacups and saucers, even if we don't use them much in everyday life. As I was born in the English country-side—I have a lovely china set passed down from my mother. Digging through the sideboard, I also found a seldom-used silver teapot, quite tarnished, but a little polish and it shined like new. Peach-painted wrought iron chairs and a small table worked perfectly, but white wicker or painted white wood would look pretty, too. Garden gazebos can be pricey, so I decided to make my own structure with a few pieces of premade, prepainted lattice from the home improvement store, as well as some posts and deck screws. To create a container garden, I gathered a bunch of terra-cotta pots that, after a coat of white paint, blended with the entire setting. And that neglected birdbath at the side of the house would also get a coat of paint and be made useful at last!

ARTIFICIAL ROSES

If you don't have roses in bloom when you're ready to entertain in your English Tea Garden, it's easy to fake it. Buy some realistic artificial roses in your color scheme (these can be found at craft stores and home décor stores), and stick a few in each rosebush. Use three to five artificial roses per bush—but make sure not to mix different colors on a single bush! (Mother Nature doesn't generally mix and match.)

ENGLISH TEA GARDEN STRUCTURE

Sledgehammer

Four post stakes

Four 8-foot 4-by-4-inch wood posts

Three 10-foot 2-by-4-inch wood posts (for the top)

Two 8-foot 2-by-4-inch wood posts (for the sides of the top)

Forty 3-inch deck screws

Electric screwdriver

Ladder

Level

1 gallon fast-drying white exterior paint

Paintbrushes

Drop cloth

Four pieces 4-by-8-foot white lattice

Two 4-foot pieces of white picket fence

Two 6-foot pieces of white picket fence

Hammer and 2-inch nails

✤ To build the structure, lay out 2-by-4s in an 8-by-10-foot rectangle on your lawn in the location you want the structure to be. Mark the four corners for the placement of the ground stakes.

✤ Drive in the post stakes with a sledgehammer at the corners of the frame.

✤ Put the 4-by-4 wood posts in the post stakes, making sure they're vertical and level.

✤ Tighten the screws in the post stakes to secure the 4-by-4s.

✤ To create the top of the structure, attach the 2-by-4s to the top of the 4-by-4s using four deck screws on each end.

✤ Attach the center brace to the middle of the two 8-foot 2-by-4s using two deck screws at each end.

✤ Paint the frame white.

✤ To attach the lattice and fencing, begin by nailing two pieces of lattice to the top in the center as a sort of roof, leaving the top sides open.

✤ Nail two pieces of lattice to the back, leaving the center open and allowing the lattice to come out on each side of the structure by one foot.

✤ Attach the two 6-foot pieces of picket fence to each back post, extending outward.

✤ Attach the two 4-foot pieces of picket fence to the back posts coming forward, creating two half walls.

(See p. 153)

7 STYLE THE SPACE   **LAY THE FOUNDATION**   The tea garden structure would look best centered on the lawn, where it could be seen and enjoyed not only from the patio but also from the kitchen window. For optimum afternoon sunlight (roses thrive in the hot sun), I faced it to the southwest. The gazebo, once built, looked terrific, but stark in the space. Adding white picket fencing on either side created a needed enclosure to the garden and extended it farther across the otherwise empty lawn. A nice fresh coat of white paint unified all the unpainted fencing, birdbath, and odd garden pots. Next, I brought in a large portable fountain and centered it inside the structure, between and in alignment with the two lattice panels, which created a "back wall." I placed the white wrought iron table and chairs to one side so the fountain wasn't hidden. The birdbath went directly across from the table to maintain a sense of balance.

SOFTEN THE LINES   Now it was time to bring in the plants and roses to create a romantic, perfumed atmosphere. First, potted rosebushes added color and texture around the wooden structure. Next, a small grouping of pots filled with white double impatiens surrounded the birdbath. The more of them I put out, the more lush and gardenlike the space began to feel. But something was still missing—the back lattice panels looked bare. No time to grow in a vine— so I wrapped some artificial ivy through the lattice, and no one could tell. Finally, I filled the large fountain with artificial peach-colored roses. You couldn't distinguish them from real flowers, so they created a long-lasting centerpiece.

PERSONALIZE WITH DETAILS   A small pedestal dish went on top of the table to give some height, and my final touches included a sprinkling of rose petals in the birdbath. I also set out some loose peach tea in a bowl to act as a potpourri.

8 STYLE THE FOOD AND TABLE   My white linen tablecloth was too large for my two-person table, so I played around a bit and finally hit upon folding it vertically to use as a runner. But no matter where I placed the napkins, the table seemed weighed down with fabric. Solution: I hung the white linens over the chair backs, and loved the effect—a liberation from tradition! Present the tea in mismatched vintage cups and saucers. Your silver flatware can have different patterns, too, for added interest and a sense of history.

APRICOT SHORTCAKES

Shortcakes

2 1/4 cups flour

1 teaspoon baking powder

5 tablespoons granulated sugar

4 1/2 ounces unsalted butter, frozen

1 large egg, beaten

1/2 cup half-and-half

1 large egg white, lightly beaten

Filling

1 1/4 cup sliced apricots mixed with
   4 tablespoons apricot jam

3/4 cup fresh whipped cream

Preheat oven to 350°.

Mix flour, baking powder, and 3 tablespoons of the sugar in a bowl. Grate the butter into the bowl and combine, using your fingers, until mixture is crumbly.

Whisk the whole egg with the cream.

Using a wooden spoon, add the egg and cream to the flour mixture a little at a time, until dough easily forms into a ball. Dough should be dry, but pliable. (If dough becomes too wet, add a small amount of flour.) Knead the dough slightly on a lightly floured board and roll gently to a thickness of about 1 inch. Using a 2-inch round cookie cutter, cut the dough into rounds and place on a

greased baking sheet. Brush tops with the egg white and sprinkle with remaining sugar.

Bake for about 25 to 30 minutes, or until golden brown. Remove from baking sheets and allow to cool on a rack.

After the shortcakes have cooled, slice them in half, horizontally. Place a spoonful of apricot mixture and a dollop of cream on bottom half and replace the top. Serve at once.

SERVES SIX

MENU
VEGETABLE TAGINE
ROASTED RED PEPPER HUMMUS WITH FLATBREAD
EXOTIC SWEETS
FAIRY FLOSS
SPICED TEA

EXOTIC OASIS

This seasonal makeover sets the stage for many magical summer evenings filled with mystery and romance.

SUMMER OFTEN CONJURES UP THOUGHTS OF TRAVEL TO FARAWAY PLACES. But what if this summer you decide you're staying home? Imagine for a moment that one of the ancient caravans of the spice trade has stopped in your own backyard. In the twilight, you hear the drivers call to one another as they unload packs and set up tents. Lanterns are hung, aromatic tea brews. As darkness falls, the tent lights up, and intricately decorated brass plates filled with sweatmeats and savory morsels are brought out one by one. A myriad of spiced fragrances float through the air as guests arrive in grand style. Surrounded by rich, sumptuous colors and cloths from exotic lands, you sit back on a cushion and share a thousand and one tales with your friends.

spice trade tents caravan sumptuous colors

EXOTIC OASIS

1 WHAT IS THE OCCASION? A party setting to be enjoyed throughout the long summer evenings.

2 ENVISION YOUR IDEAL SETTING A lavish setting on the lawn, rich in color and dramatic in mood. It would transport guests to a faraway place without their ever leaving the backyard and could also be used for smaller get-togethers after its stunning debut.

3 DEVELOP A MAKEOVER STYLE I've always used lots of ethnic textiles and styling supplies—everything from silk saris to hand-painted pottery. Inspired by a Moorish lantern that made me think of date palms and spice markets, a photo in my Style File of a nomad's tent draped with curtains, and the first hot days of summer, I decided on an "Exotic Oasis" style.

FABRIC DRAPE

60 yards orange fabric
60 yards mustard fabric
Yellow silk sari or other long piece of contrasting fabric
Hammer, tacker, or staple gun
Ladder

❀ Build the basic gazebo structure, as described in the "English Tea Garden" makeover.

❀ Paint the structure an earth tone or leave it natural.

❀ Don't precut your fabric. Working side to side, starting in the front, begin by draping one color of fabric over the structure to create a roof. Allow it to drop all the way down to the ground on each side.

❀ Staple the fabric at the top to secure it, then cut off the extra fabric at the bottom, leaving it loose to flow in the wind or be gathered at each post.

❀ Next to the piece you've already secured, repeat the procedure with the other color of fabric. Continue draping, stapling, and cutting, alternating the colors, until you've covered the top and two sides with fabric. One round should do it.

❀ Next, starting at the two front corners of the structure, drape one piece of material up and over the structure to the back, letting about one foot hang over the side of the frame, creating an apron on each side. This piece should touch the ground in the front and back as well.

❀ Working inward in the front, place another piece of material, front to back, right next to the one that is hanging over the sides.

❀ In the front, staple one piece of material horizontally to mimic the apron on the sides. Pull it up in two places in the front and staple to create a draped effect. Let this material hang to the ground as well on each side, covering the two front posts.

❀ Swag a contrasting fabric (I used the sari) over one corner in the front, and staple (optional).

❀ You can let the material sway in the breeze and hang for more privacy, or tie it loosely around each post to open up the view.

4 CREATE YOUR STYLE BOARD   From my box of fabric swatches I pulled one in a rich orange and attached it to my board. Next came tear sheets of grasses, desert plants, and palms. As I flipped through a food magazine, a few exotic recipes caught my eye, and I pulled them out and pinned them up to start playing with flavor ideas for my feast.

5 PAINT YOUR COLOR PALETTE   Sahara Sunset and Turmeric Yellow. I found one of these colors in the most unexpected place—the spice rack! The yellow of turmeric powder seemed to speak to me in an exotic tongue, so I poured some of the spice into a plastic bag to pin to my Style Board. You never know where inspiration might come from!

STYLING SUPPLY LIST

Materials to build the structure (see Style-To)	Papyrus
Wooden pallets for seating area	Flax plants
Lounge chair	Protea
Brass table	Copper, wood, and silver accessories
Old kilim rugs	Candles
Large orange seat cushions	Moroccan tea glasses
Copper urns	Burlap
Sheer fabric in rich, exotic hues	Metal lanterns
Silk sari	Tagine clay pot
Ethnic pillows	

6 GATHER YOUR STYLING SUPPLIES   A yellow sari worked well with my color palette and also underlined the faraway-places theme. Next, I gathered up unrelated objects that matched the color palette or aligned with my theme: a few pillows, some richly colored candles, an assortment of old kilim rugs and runners, and various copper and wood trays, urns, and dishes. I kept my gathering confined to those items with an ethnic feel, daydreaming of Arabian nights and the Taj Majal with each item.

Finding the right fabric was the real trick for creating my casbah tent. It needed to withstand the outdoors, be inexpensive, and drape like a charm. I found the perfect polyester bolts at a discount fabric store (always a useful source for your styling projects). Materials for building the structure

are available at the home improvement store. You may even be able to pick up some wooden pallets for the seating area at your local grocery store.

7 STYLE THE SPACE   **LAY THE FOUNDATION**   This step begins with the assembly of the structure (see Style-To in English Tea Garden, p. 159). There was a lovely oak tree on the lawn with tremendous character that I thought would make a wonderful backdrop (sure, you've seen oak trees in the desert), so I positioned the structure in front of it, then created a "floor" and "sofa" with wooden pallets (see Style-To, below). A brass table in the center provided a spot for our feast, and a lounge chair next to the entryway extended the space forward and offered a spot for solitary dreaming.

PALLET SEATING AREA

8 wooden pallets
One 10 foot 2 x 4
Saw
Hammer and nails
Throw rugs
8 large cushions
Accent pillows

For the pallet floor:

❀ Lay three of the pallets on the ground in a row along the backside of the structure. Place two more pallets in front of the row to create a u-shaped floor. (There will be an open area left in the center of the floor for later placement of the table.)

For the pallet sofa:

❀ Cut one of the pallets in half. Place each pallet half adjacent to each other on top of the back row of floor pallets. This will serve as the sofa seat.

❀ The remaining two pallets will be used to make the back of the sofa.* Place the pallets upright behind the back row of floor pallets, aligning with the sofa seat. Nail the 2 x 4 to the rear posts of the structure, as well as to the sofa backs to hold in place.

*Note: You may need to cut the palettes down to fit the size of your cushions.

❀ Cover the pallets with the rugs, and place the seat cushions and accent pillows.

SOFTEN THE LINES The soft styling would set the entire tone for this tentlike space, starting with the draping of the fabric to put the tent in place (see Style-To, p. 166). I covered the pallets with the kilim rugs to soften the hard wood, then placed eight matching large cushions that I bought for a steal as the base and back of the "sofa." You could achieve the same effect with sofa cushions or any other type, even unmatched, covered with a bedspread or throw. You could also make the sofa from two large pieces of foam (purchased at an upholstery or fabric store) covered with heavy fabric. Bright decorative pillows finished it off. I laid down several more rugs to extend the encampment and create a pathway into my haven, then placed two large flax plants on either side for a dramatic entrance. A grouping of papyrus in pots wrapped in burlap suggested exotic lands and established the camp's far edge.

PERSONALIZE WITH DETAILS There would be no bright flashlights in this desert tent! I needed a subtle lighting scheme to set the mood and drive the darkness out to the party's perimeter. I hung the metal Moorish candle lantern directly above the table with a heavy rope. A variety of candles, in lanterns and set up in groups, gave a warm glow. (If you can't find enough lanterns, make some by placing candles in waxed paper bags with sand at the bottom.)

8 STYLE THE FOOD AND TABLE Pull out rustic metal dishes, pottery, and wooden bowls for your table set-up. Mismatch them for maximum caravan effect, offering one guest vegetable tagine and couscous on a small aluminum platter, and another the same meal in a wooden bowl. The hummus can be purchased and served in a dish surrounded by rolled flatbread. Add a dash of olive oil on top and a sprinkle of paprika. Set out a rustic metal bowl heaped with spices—cumin, curry, cloves, turmeric, and cinnamon all work well. The colors and textures intensify the exotic atmosphere, and the aromas complement your meal. An extra piece of fabric can double as a tablecloth, accenting the brass table and creating a vibrant backdrop for the food.

BURLAP papyrus **kilim rugs** candle lantern

FAIRY FLOSS

This exotic snack, similar to cotton candy, is available at ethnic food markets. I pulled out a handful, placed it in a silver bowl, twisted it into a peak, and topped it with a star anise. Fairy floss's sculptural qualities allow for an array of styling possibilities. Try using it to create a large edible sculpture on a buffet!

EXOTIC TREATS

Look in ethnic grocery and gourmet shops for treats like nougat, Turkish Delight and sesame bars.

VEGETABLE TAGINE

2–3 teaspoons whole cumin seeds

1 cup yellow split peas, rinsed

1 cup shallots, quartered

2 garlic cloves, peeled and minced

4 cups vegetable stock

1/2 each yellow, red, and green pepper, seeded
   and cut into strips

1 medium sweet potato, peeled and chopped

2 cups diced tomatoes, canned or fresh

1 cup baby carrots, peeled and left whole

1 cup baby turnips (can substitute 1 medium
   turnip chopped)

3 tablespoons lemon juice

20 dried apricot halves, finely sliced

1 cup dry white wine

1/4 teaspoon ground ginger

1/4 teaspoon ground cinnamon

1 teaspoon cayenne pepper

2 teaspoons honey

8 cups cooked couscous, prepared according to
   package directions

Toast cumin in oven at 300° for approximately 5 minutes, or until dark brown, tossing halfway through cooking time. Set aside.

In a large saucepan, combine yellow peas, shallots, and garlic. Add stock and bring to a boil. Cover, reduce heat, and simmer for 20 minutes. Add the remaining ingredients (except the couscous) and again bring to a boil. Reduce heat and allow to simmer for another 20 to 25 minutes, or until vegetables are cooked.

Place one cup of couscous on each plate and top with a spoonful of tagine. Sprinkle each serving with toasted cumin seeds.

SERVES EIGHT

175

CHAMPAGNE WEDDING

*This wedding makeover is a backyard fairy tale come true for the bride and groom
looking for celebratory style on a budget.*

DO YOU DREAM OF A WEDDING DAY SO SERENE THAT THE RADIANT BRIDE SKIPS BAREFOOT IN THE SOFT SUMMER GRASS? In this classic garden setting, the elegance of rich, tailored green brocade and a froth of white tulle form a lush but sophisticated backdrop for bride and groom. Guests in summer hats and linen suits are in attendance; tears of joy gleam in the sunlight for a moment before dissolving in the soft summer breeze. Family and friends raise champagne glasses to toast the happy couple, and children in party clothes begin an impromptu game on the lawn as the wedding cakes are cut. With the blue sky arcing overhead, a few puffy clouds masquerading as angels, birds swooping and singing, and the fragrance of flowers in the air, it seems as if all heaven and earth are blessing the sacred union.

soft wedding white radiant serenity grassy green

1 WHAT IS THE OCCASION?   A summer wedding ceremony and cake reception.

2 ENVISION YOUR IDEAL SETTING   An elegant backyard wedding for a bride and groom with a limited budget but sophisticated, contemporary tastes. No fussiness in the decorations with this wedding. The setting had to merit a formal, dressy affair, with a canopy of some kind and an altar to focus attention on the ceremony. On one hand, the space should comfortably accommodate at least 50 guests, and on the other, it should have charming small details to delight the eye.

3 DEVELOP A MAKEOVER STYLE   In many ways, a wedding already has a style—love, marriage, present and future family. I didn't want to add any gimmicks to the nuptials, but I did want an image to help unify my styling. Looking through my Style File, I came across a magazine tearsheet of a bride and groom toasting with delicate champagne glasses. I immediately thought "Champagne Wedding."

WEDDING STRUCTURE FABRIC DRAPE

See English Tea Garden makeover for materials list and instructions for the structure.

Twelve 10-by-4-foot pieces of white tulle (six for each of the sides)

Two 27-foot lengths of 5-foot-wide white cotton

One 11-by-four-foot piece of grass-green fabric for the front valance

Hammer tacker, or staple gun

Hammer and about twenty 3-inch nails or tent stakes

❀ Starting on one side of the structure at the front, gather a piece of tulle and staple or tack it to the top side rails, leaving six inches of netting above the rail and the remainder falling to the ground.

❀ Secure the tulle to the ground with tent stakes or nails pushed into the ground.

❀ Repeat this approximately six times on each side, or until both sides are completely covered. The front and back will be open.

❀ Next, working front to back, drape the pieces of cotton over the top of the structure so that it makes a roof and hangs to the ground on both sides. Make sure the extra 6 inches of netting that is along the top rails is pushed to the inside of the structure when you place the cotton on top. This will hide the top rail and create a ruffle along the inside for a more finished look. Pull the cotton taut over the top and staple it down around the perimeter so it doesn't float up with the wind.

❀ To complete the roof, attach the second piece of cotton from the center crossbeam to the back. Secure with staples all around the top. Allow the extra cotton to hang over the back, creating a flap, and pull the flap taut. Secure with staples.

❀ Depending on your preference and current wind conditions, you can either leave the cotton loose on the sides or staple it to the structure and nail it to the ground, as with the netting.

❀ Now fold the green material in half so that it's about 2 feet wide. Staple it along the top rail in the front, making sure to keep it even as you go. Wrap the ends around each side post, cut off any extra, fold over, and staple so it looks clean from the front.

4 CREATE YOUR STYLE BOARD I started with a photograph of a white Casablanca lily. Its simplicity was certainly an embodiment of less-is-more beauty, and I loved the contrasting colors of the green pistil surrounded by soft white petals. I went to the fabric store for samples and tacked up white-and-green material that matched the flower. A photo of a summer porch furnished in wicker with green cushions appealed to me—it wasn't a wedding, but the color combination was lovely. I added some pictures of homemade wedding cakes and small but striking bouquets. A length of white satin ribbon and some tulle finished off my creative collage.

STYLING SUPPLY LIST

Materials to build the structure (see Style-To)

Narrow table or console

Small round table

Cement blocks

White chairs

PVC pipe and finials

White tulle, cotton, and satin ribbons

Green brocade or embossed fabric

An assortment of white flowers, such as Casablanca lilies and stock

White vases

Lemon leaves and baby's tears

White candles

White cake pedestals

Cake plates and silver forks

Champagne glasses

Silver ice bucket

Large moss balls

5 PAINT YOUR COLOR PALETTE Wedding White and Grassy Green, both from the lily.

6 GATHER YOUR STYLING SUPPLIES Tables for the altar and cake should be easy to find, as you can adapt any number of sizes and shapes to suit—and they needn't match, because you will later drape them with fabric. I used a round table for the food and an old office table for the main altar. Rather than rent an arch or gazebo at enormous cost, I decided to build one, complete with a distinctive aisle for the bride to make her grand entrance. These two projects would involve nothing more than a trip to the home improvement store, an afternoon with a hammer and nails, and a strong friend to help. I found white tulle and some lovely green brocade at the fabric store and did some comparison-shopping at florists before ordering flowers and

champagne glasses **summer hats** classic garden

greens for a few key spots. You can buy moss balls at a dry floral goods store or make your own by gluing sphagnum moss to large Styrofoam balls and then spraying them lightly with green paint to even out the color. White vases and white candles can be bought and borrowed, which leaves only the chairs to rent.

7 STYLE THE SPACE   **LAY THE FOUNDATION** I started by building and painting the gazebo structure (see Style-To for English Tea Garden, p. 159), then centered it and set it back far enough on the lawn to allow room for chairs and a processional aisle, but with enough space behind it to make the altar table accessible from both the front and back. Next, I centered the altar table under the gazebo, setting it on cement blocks for extra height. When the chairs arrived, I set them up in rows facing the structure, leaving an aisle that I lined with finial posts (see Style-To, below) at the ends of the first three rows. I placed the round table off to the side for serving at the reception.

FINIAL POSTS

The length of your walkway will determine how many posts you need. This makes six posts.

Six 30-inch lengths of ¹/₂-inch galvanized water pipe

Six 3-foot lengths of Schedule 40 PVC 1-inch water pipe

6 wood ball finials with 1-inch base and a metal screw-in bottom to go over PVC pipe

6 Schedule 40 PVC 1-inch caps

Fast-drying white exterior paint (enough to cover your finial posts)

Sledgehammer

Electric drill (with a bit slightly smaller than the screw on the bottom of the finials)

Flowers or greens for small bouquets (one bouquet per post)

2-inch-wide white satin ribbon (enough to connect all the posts together)

1-inch-wide white satin ribbon (about 1 foot per bouquet, per post)

❀ Before you construct the finial posts, you'll need to paint the PVC pipe, the caps, and the wood finials white and allow them to dry.

❀ Drill a hole in the center of each PVC cap and screw a ball finial onto each.

❀ Twist one cap and finial onto each PVC pipe.

❀ Using the sledgehammer, drive each galvanized pipe place into the ground where you want your posts.

❀ Slide one PVC pipe with attached finial over each piece of galvanized pipe.

❀ Drape the 2-inch ribbon between the posts and tie around the base of each finial.

❀ To make your bouquets, gather a small amount of greens or flowers and tie together with a foot-long piece of 1-inch ribbon. Do not cut the ends of the ribbon; use them to tie the bouquet onto the finished post.

SOFTEN THE LINES Now that the bare bones were in place, I covered the wooden structure with fabric (see Style-To, p. 178), creating a tailored valance with the brocaded green fabric and white tulle curtains for the posts. I draped the altar table with white cotton fabric for the base and green fabric on top to provide a two-tone base for the white candles and vases. The serving table got a layer of white cotton, topped with a piece of light green tulle.

PERSONALIZE WITH DETAILS I made six small swags of baby's tears and tied each one to a finial post with white satin ribbon, draping the ribbon from one finial post to the next to make a cordon (see Style-To, p. 183). Moss balls defined the entrance to the aisle. The altar was styled with minimalist arrangements of individual stems of white flowers—lilies and stock—in several long-necked white glass vases of various heights. Assorted white candles in three different sizes went in the middle of the altar, which was also adorned with glossy green lemon leaves and a few more white lilies. I was careful to keep the altar simple so that it could quickly be converted to a cake-cutting table after the ceremony.

8 STYLE THE FOOD AND TABLE Rather than stacking the cake in a traditional fashion, I decided to keep each one separate, as it aligned best with my simplistic theme. I served the cakes on pedestals and adorned at the last minute with freshly cut flowers. Keep the flowers in the same color palette as your makeover—you may even have some left over from your table styling! Place a single large flower in the center of one or two cakes, while using a grouping of smaller flowers around the base and sides for another. For a variation of a typical champagne toast, garnish each glass by placing a fresh raspberry or strawberry in the glass before pouring champagne or sliding the fruit onto the rim.

ALTAR TABLE

1 tall, narrow table

Cinder blocks (to raise table height if needed)

*Cotton fabric in white and green**

6 long-necked white vases in varying heights

Fresh flowers and lemon leaves

8 white candles (one or two pillars each in 3, 6, and 9-inch heights)

Double-sided craft tape

Large safety pins

*Note: The amount of fabric will depend upon the size of your table. Make sure you have enough white fabric to create a full-length tablecloth, and enough green fabric to hang approximately halfway to the ground on all sides.

❋ Drape the table evenly with the white fabric. (If you need to use two or more pieces of fabric to create a full-length tablecloth, simply tape the pieces together and to the table with double-sided tape. The tape line will not be visible once layered with the second piece of fabric.)

❋ Next, make sure the fabric puddles on the ground and tuck under the edges. Weigh down the fabric edges with a rock or weights, if you anticipate breezy weather.

❋ Lay the green fabric on top and adjust so that it hangs approximately halfway to the ground. Be sure to create a straight, even edge. Secure the green fabric to the white fabric using safety pins or tape.

❋ Arrange the vases on each side of the table in groupings of three or four. Place the tallest toward the back, and the shortest in front, and fill with single stems of white flowers.

❋ Group the candles (use a variety of sizes all in the same color) in the center of the table and scatter with fresh lemon leaves and flowers. Simple, quick, and extremely elegant!

(See p. 181)

WEDDING CAKE WITH RASPBERRY FILLING AND BUTTER CREAM FROSTING

9 cups all-purpose flour

8 teaspoons baking powder

4 teaspoons baking soda

2 teaspoons salt

12 large eggs, room temperature

10 tablespoons vanilla extract

3 cups unsalted butter, softened

5 1/2 cups sugar

4 1/2 cups plus 6 tablespoons sour cream

4 tablespoons vegetable oil

1/2 cup whipping cream

Filling

4 cups raspberry preserves

Butter Cream Frosting (see recipe)

Position 1 rack in top third of oven and 1 rack in lowest third of oven and preheat to 325. Butter one 6-inch by 3-inch cake pan, one 9-inch by 3-inch cake pan, and one 12-inch by 3-inch cake pan. Line bottoms with parchment paper.

Sift 4 1/2 cups flour, 4 teaspoons baking powder, 2 teaspoons baking soda and 1 teaspoon salt into large bowl. In separate bowl, whisk 6 eggs and 5 tablespoons vanilla.

With an electric mixer, cream 1 1/2 cups butter and 2 3/4 cups sugar until light and fluffy, stopping occasionally to scrape down sides of bowl, about 3 minutes. Add 2 1/4 plus 3 tablespoons sour cream and beat until smooth, about 20 seconds. Reduce speed to low. Add dry ingredients and beat just until blended, about 30 seconds; do not overbeat. Gradually beat in 2 tablespoons oil. Add egg mixture and beat just until blended. Add 1/4 cup whipping cream and beat just until combined, about 15 seconds. Spoon 1 1/4 cups batter into 6-inch pan, 3 1/2 cups batter into 9-inch pan and remaining batter into 12-inch pan. Smooth tops.

Place 12-inch cake pan on lowest oven rack and 9-inch and 6-inch pans on upper rack. Bake cakes until tester inserted into center comes out clean; about 35 minutes for 6-inch cake, 45 minutes for 9-inch cake and 1 hour for 12-inch cake (cakes will not rise to tops of pans).

Transfer cakes to racks and cool completely. Run small sharp knife around pan sides to loosen cakes. Turn cakes out onto waxed paper-lined work surface and set aside. With remaining ingredients, make second batch of batter as described above. Bake cakes, cool, and unmold following the same instructions.

BUTTER CREAM FROSTING

(You will need to make two batches to frost all cakes.)

2 cups unsalted butter, room temperature

3 3/4 cups powdered sugar

2 1/2 cups plus 2 tablespoons whipping cream

1 tablespoon vanilla extract

With an electric mixer, cream butter and sugar on low speed until light and fluffy, about 2 minutes. Increase speed to medium-high and beat until frosting whitens slightly, about 2 minutes. Reduce speed to medium. Gradually beat in 1 cup cream. Continue beating for 1 minute. Mix 1 tablespoon vanilla into 1 cup cream. Gradually beat cream mixture into frosting. Increase speed to medium-high and beat until fluffy, about 5 minutes. Reduce speed to medium. Add remaining 1/2 cup plus 2 tablespoons cream and beat until fluffy, about 15 minutes. (You may add food coloring now, if desired. To achieve the pale green shown in photo, use 7 drops yellow food coloring, and 4 drops green.)

Transfer frosting to large bowl. Cover and set aside; do not refrigerate.

ASSEMBLY

Using serrated knife, cut each cake horizontally in half. Place one 6-inch cake, cut side up on plate. Spread with 1/4 cup of preserves. Top with second 6-inch cake layer, cut side up. Spread with 1/2 cup white frosting. Continue alternating layers with preserves and frosting until all four 6-inch cake layers are added. Spread 1/2 cup white frosting over top and sides of cake. Repeat process with 9-inch cake layers using 1/2 cup plus 3 tablespoons raspberry preserves and 1 cup frosting for each layer. Cover top and sides with 3/4 cup plus 2 tablespoons frosting. Repeat process again with 12-inch cake layers, using 1 cup plus 1 tablespoon preserves and 2 1/2 cups frosting for each layer. Spread 1 cup frosting over top and sides of cake.

Chill all cakes until frosting sets, about 1 hour. (Can be made ahead. Wrap cakes tightly and chill 4 days or freeze up to 2 weeks. Thaw frozen cakes in refrigerator overnight before continuing.)

Bring cake to room temperature before serving and decorate with fresh Casablanca lilies.

SERVES FIFTY

CONCLUSION

As the poet Tennyson said,

'Tis better to have loved and lost,

Than never to have loved at all."

Well . . . maybe that's a bit melodramatic if we're talking about styling, but the same spirit applies to any creative endeavor. As the poet Coelho says,

"Better to have styled and made a few mistakes,

Than never to have styled at all."

Okay, so I'm not a poet. But you get the idea.

Fear of failure is the main reason some people never undertake creative challenges. But I'm a firm believer in facing one's fears. What's wonderful about styling is that no experiment really ends up in failure. Even if it doesn't turn out as well as you expected, you'll still feel exhilarated for having tried, for having made progress, and for knowing better what to do next time. It's funny how once you tackle styling, all those initial fears of failure tend to shrink to laughable specks. Just like anything worthwhile in life, styling takes getting involved, diving in, relishing the challenge—and changing things as you find better ways to accomplish them.

If you have paged through this book and still feel you are lacking the confidence to begin styling, start with small projects. Throw a lunch for a couple of close friends rather than a dinner for twelve; style one table before tackling the whole room. Soon, what once looked daunting will start to exhilarate you, and you will see that styling is really quite simple and enjoyable once you give it a chance.

I hope that with this book I have given you lots of useful ideas and a step-by-step method of putting

them into action. I also hope I've helped to reinvigorate your creativity, inspire your esthetic sensibilities, and

free your inner artist. But most of all, with this book I wish to give you the gift my mother gave to me—

a life filled with style! ❧

"Keep creating . . . that's the joy of life!"

RESOURCE LIST

INDOORS

Anthropologie

800-309-2500

www.anthropologie.com

An original mix of accessories, furniture, and gifts.

Art of Morocco

310-659-9026

www.artofmorocco.com

Ethnic home accessories.

Big Daddy's Antiques

800-517-3883

www.bdantiques.com

Vintage pieces for the home and garden.

Charles & Charles

310-559-0138

www.charlesandcharles.com

Antique and reproduction furniture.

Chest N Drawers

323-938-1566

www.chestndrawers.com

European and American vintage textiles.

Con-Tact Brand

877-353-6410

www.contactbrand.com

Great adhesive papers for all uses!

Crate & Barrel

800-996-9960

www.crateandbarrel.com

Great seasonal items and basics for the home.

Dare Crackers

www.15minutestofame.com

Delicious crackers and cookies.

Department 56, Inc.

800-548-8696

www.department56.com

Seasonal accessories and collectibles.

eBay.com

www.ebay.com

Online marketplace for home wares.

Fedora Products

213-487-4073

www.botanicalprintsoncanvas.com

Beautiful canvas prints.

Garden Ridge

832-391-7204

www.gardenridge.com

The home decor and craft marketplace.

Kier Designs

310-487-2487

Beautiful vintage lamps and frames.

Homework

323-466-1153

www.homeworkbrand.com

Unusual and colorful modern furniture and accessories.

IKEA

800 434-IKEA

www.ikea.com

Affordable solutions for better living.

Jonathan Adler

800-657-7752

www.jonathanadler.com

Mid-century-inspired pottery, lighting, furniture, and textiles.

La Brea Antique Collection

323-938-9444

Modern furnishings and accessories from the 1950s, '60s, and '70s.

Maison Midi

323-935-3157

European housewares.

Nellie Anne's Collectables

949-631-1852

Colorful vintage furnishings and accessories.

Pottery Barn

800-922-5507

www.potterybarn.com

Great linens, pillows, accessories, and seasonal items for the home.

Romancing the Home

323-935-9811

Romantic home and garden furniture and accessories.